UNDERSTANDING CONTEMPORA...

THE ISSUES BENEATH THE SURFACE

UNDERSTANDING CONTEMPORARY ISLAMIC CRISES IN THE MIDDLE EAST

THE ISSUES BENEATH THE SURFACE

Graham E. Fuller

LEIDEN PUBLICATIONS

Cover design: Tarek Atrissi Design
Cover image: Sheikh Zayed Grand Mosque Centre, Abu Dhabi, © Tarek Atrissi
Lay-out: CO2 Premedia

ISBN   978 90 8728 267 7
e-ISBN 978 94 0060 268 7 (ePDF)
e-ISBN 978 94 0060 269 4 (ePUB)
NUR   717

© Graham E. Fuller / Leiden University Press, 2016

This book is distributed in North America by the University of Chicago Press (www.press.uchicago.edu).

Foreword

Ever since the 2011 'Arab Spring' erupted, many places in the Middle East and North Africa have been in crisis. Often, these crises are explained with references to Islam, for example to the Sunni-Shia divide, or Islamic extremism sponsored from Saudi Arabia or Iran. Such explanations are often one-sided and superficial, and in the public debate well-informed balanced views of what goes on beneath the surface are rare. Graham Fuller is an exception. His vast experience in the Middle East and subsequent writing projects have made him a highly respected scholar and speaker on political Islam and the Middle East in a wide sense. In Spring 2016 he came to Leiden at our invitation to give a series of lectures which formed the basis of this book. The lectures attracted many students, academics, government officials and NGO activists and led to lively discussions and new insights for those present. We are confident that this book will also finds its way to a wide readership.

Jan Michiel Otto Van Vollenhoven
Institute for Law,
Governance, and Society
VVI

Petra Sijpesteijn
Leiden – Center for the study
of Islam and Society
LUCIS

Contents

Power and Identity in Muslim World Politics

PART ONE: NON-RELIGIOUS CONSIDERATIONS
IN THE POLITICS OF SHARI'A

What is the appropriate role, if any, of Shari'a law in the politics and govern-ance of the Muslim world? This question occupies a major place in the polit-ical thinking of all Muslims, regardless of their response. It is also a focus of Western academic study as more Muslims migrate to the West, many with positive views of the place of Shari'a in Muslim life.

The West may find the centrality of the Shari'a issue to be difficult to under-stand, viewing it as if it represents some kind of throwback to seemingly "medieval" conceptions of law linked to religion. Yet within the Muslim world the reasons for the importance of Shari'a are not hard to discern. First of all—unlike in the West where Shari'a as a body of religious principles and rulings is perceived by many as dated, negative, and inappropriate to a more modern and secular world—in the Muslim world the concept of Shari'a is a strongly positive one. The word Shari'a itself derives from the Arabic root for "path" or "way"; it suggests a broad and generalized notion resembling in part the use of the term "The Way" in other religious traditions, including Christianity and Buddhism. It represents a quest to create a society in which people live in accordance with God's will and law, thereby perhaps attaining divine grace. In this sense, then, Shari'a can be perceived as above all a con-cept, something more than just a specific body of prescriptive laws. As such, Muslims see Shari'a as representing the core of their faith, an expression of the moral and legal framework within which to live on earth. For most Mus-lims it represents a positive virtue worthy of embracing.

Shari'a, therefore, represents the core of Islamic faith and culture that seeks to codify the principles of the Islamic faith as derived from its two key

9

sources: the *Qur'an* and the *Hadith*. The Qur'an of course represents direct divine revelation to the Prophet Muhammad; it particularly treats such grand issues as the nature of God, as well as the nature of relations between God and Man. Doing so, it offers only limited guidance by way of specifics on law or governance. The Hadith, on the other hand, represent an attempt to recall and record the words and the deeds of the Prophet during his lifetime as leader of the new Muslim community. It deals with the experience of the Prophet in executing early governance in accordance with his understanding of the Qur'an. In this sense the Hadith are much more specific on issues of social organization and governance than the Qur'an, though not yet fully codified into law. The words and deeds of the Prophet were recorded perhaps beginning only one hundred years after the Prophet's death; as a result there has always been some degree of legal controversy about the accuracy of what was ultimately recorded.

So what, then, is Shari'a? Shari'a could be best defined as a human (not divine) process on the part of Islamic scholars to codify a legal system based on the divine sources of the Qur'an and the non-divine records of Hadith. It is a flexible and living tradition as interpreted (in differing ways) by Shari'a courts across the Muslim world.

Now, Shari'a law—indeed any body of law—cannot be implemented without the existence of a State of some kind. A State implies the existence of authority, a body capable of determining the legal interpretations of Shari'a, in addition to possessing the power to impose it upon society. The full adoption and application of Shari'a is, at least in principle, a key goal of most Islamist movements and Islamic parties.

As Professor Jan Michiel Otto has pointed out, there are at least two aspects to Shari'a: First is the realm of *personal law* that involves issues of personal behavior, private morality, family law relating to marriage, divorce, sexuality, hygiene, issues of inheritance, and the like. The implementation of various aspects of personal law—in different ways depending upon locale and tradition—has a long history in Muslim societies. Traditionally, its validity finds fairly ready acceptance within Muslim societies, even if its actual details might be disputed and/or evolving. The second aspect of Shari'a is its relationship to the State, involving issues of state powers, lawmaking, legislation, citizenship, public morality, relations with other states both Muslim and non-Muslim, and the place of minorities and non-Muslims.

As in so many things, once we move beyond the conceptual and philosophical understanding of Shari'a and delve into details, areas of controversy emerge. Furthermore, as the *politics* around the adoption of Shari'a evolve, it becomes evident that far more than mere religious factors are involved in the debate around the place of Shari'a.

★ ★ ★

There is a large body of scholarship dealing with the religious and theological aspects of Shari'a and its historical evolution. Human society being what it is, however, a large number of *non-religious factors* likewise influence the politics surrounding the role of Shari'a and its adoption in Muslim societies.

This essay seeks to examine some of the key *non-religious* factors that impact the perception and role of Shari'a in the politics of the Muslim world as well as the life of Muslims in the West. I focus particular attention here upon the factors of *identity politics* and *power relations* in Muslim thinking about Islamism and Islamist politics.

In these regards, further definition is in order. I define *Islamism* (and, consequently, Islamists) rather broadly—consistent, in my view, with the reality of its many varieties on the ground. Thus, an *Islamist* is someone who believes that the Qur'an and the Hadith have vital things to say about Islamic society and governance, and who seeks to apply these concepts in some way to society and governance.

The breadth of this definition therefore embraces a *spectrum* of Muslim political thinking and practice from the moderate to the radical, the conservative to the liberal, the contemporary to the traditional, the non-violent to the violent; it further recognizes degrees of acceptance of elements of democratic principles in contemporary governance. Naturally, discussion of the place of Shari'a figures immediately into such a range of considerations. Moreover, *how* the principles of Shari'a should be introduced into governance becomes a natural topic of debate: whether it should be via force, by exhortation (*da'wa*), through a political party, or by way of an ideological movement.

Some neo-conservative (even Islamophobic) ideological thinkers in the West such as Daniel Pipes in the US, Martin Kramer in Israel, Geert Wilders in the Netherlands, or Ayaan Ali Hirsi, treat Islamism as being *by definition* a distinctly dangerous phenomenon that needs to be eliminated; for them Islamism is synonymous with fascism, aggression, violence, and dictatorship. While these features can and indeed have characterized some Islamist movements, the spectrum of Islamist movements is far broader than these narrow and frozen characterizations. They leave no room for political and intellectual *evolution*—the heart of the issue in analyzing contemporary Islamism. Indeed, we cannot analytically end up characterizing Islamism by definition in strictly negative terms; some Islamist parties have had some real successes and show encouraging ideological evolution. These movements cannot be excluded from the spectrum of Islamism simply because they do not meet the negative criteria cited above.

Islamism also deserves a great deal of attention simply because it is the single most important movement for change and reform in the Muslim world; no other movements rival it in numerical support. The reasons are clear: Islamists have been the overwhelmingly dominant group in Muslim society who have criticized the shortcomings of existing regimes in the Muslim world, especially for regime failure to implement Islamic values and Islamic law, for their corruption, frequent hypocrisy in their lifestyles (especially in Saudi Arabia), oppression, absence of social justice, and subservience to the West. They have demanded reforms and spoken out against rulers. They have been arrested, imprisoned, tortured, executed, silenced over many decades and hence have acquired a degree of credibility and respect that few other political leaders have ever attained. They furthermore speak in the vocabulary of Muslim culture, the familiar cultural framework of Muslim society—and not within some Western framework of political values. They have above all acquired a degree of trust within large elements of Muslim society.

The Functional Characteristics of Islamism
Islamists are thus active participants within society—and in politics, where permitted. Their ideologies aside, though, what are the main *functional char-*

acteristics of Islamist action within society and politics? (Not all Islamists will necessarily agree on these goals, but these objectives tend to predominate. In addition, this list is not necessarily by prioritization.)

First, Islamists seek the elimination of regimes not viewed as properly Islamic on the basis of the many criticisms leveled against such regimes over the years. There is no consensus among Islamists on how to get rid of such regimes—whether by democratic process (if such exists and could actually implement change), or through social movements to pressure regimes, or through acts of violence that would overthrow such regimes. (We should also note that tactical disagreement on these issues also characterizes non-Islamic political opposition as well.)

Clearly any effort to bring about regime change entails great risks to the actors involved, particularly if they contemplate using force. And many have advocated the use of force in the past, either because peaceful or democratic means were of no avail against harsh and authoritarian regimes, or because they rejected the democratic process on principle.

Second, nearly all Islamist movements speak of the need to establish an Islamic State. But the term is rarely defined in any meaningful way, except to refer to application of Shari'a law as a key litmus test. Even here, however, different formulations are used: Is Shari'a to be understood as the primary source of legislation, or as the sole source of legislation, or as one (of many) source(s) of legislation? Among these formulations there is much room for interpretation. Of course even "application of Shari'a" is itself an imprecise term. Yet advocating the establishment of an "Islamic State" seems to be a nominal prerequisite for most but not all Islamist movements.

Third, some Islamist movements aspire to restore the institution of the Caliphate. Indeed, the Caliphate is viewed by most Muslims as richly symbolic of the unity and power of Islamic authority across Islamic history. "Caliph" (Khalifa in Arabic) simply means "successor"—in this case denoting the successor to the Prophet after his death; yet in this case "successor" is understood not as a prophet (for there can be no more prophets in Islam) but as leader of the new Muslim community and state in the years after the Prophet's death. The institution of the Caliphate has risen and fallen in significance in

Islamic history, disappearing over certain periods, while strongly resuscitated later in the Ottoman Empire as an expression of the centralized religious authority of the Ottomans.

It is significant that in 1923 Mustafa Kemal Atatürk, the founder of the new Turkish Republic, abolished the office of the Caliphate as an institution no longer of value to his aspirations for a strictly secular Turkey. Nonetheless, Turkey had no real "right" to abolish the office simply because Caliphs had resided in Turkey for the last several hundred years. It was as if the prime minister of Italy would one day arbitrarily decide to abolish the Papacy on his own, without consultation or consideration of the views of tens of millions of Catholics around the world who would not agree to the step. The abolition of the Caliphate was thus perceived by many Muslims as shocking, illegal and damaging to the worldwide Islamic community (or "umma").

Some Islamists still see the eventual restoration of the office of the Caliphate as a significant symbol of progress towards Islamic unity. Such an office could also provide a centralized religious focus (as with the Pope in Christianity), a place where authoritative religious pronouncements could be made on behalf of the umma. Yet most Muslims also recognize that the problems of resuscitating the Caliphate today are daunting. Who would he be, how would he be selected, what would be his authorities over Muslims, how binding would his religious interpretations be, what would be the nature of his authorities over Muslim heads of state in other countries, or over other national clerics and muftis? Achieving consensus on these questions is nearly impossible today.

Several Islamist movements, most notably the "Islamic State" (Da'ish, ISIS, ISIL), advocate the restoration of the Caliphate—and ISIS actually did proclaim that restoration on its own territory. Other groups like Hizb ut-Tahrir (Hizb al-Tahrir or Liberation Party) have drawn up lengthy blueprints for the establishment of a Caliphate, though not yet implemented. Few Muslim states have advocated strongly for the restoration of the office as a priority for the Muslim world. Nonetheless, the concept has considerable emotional and cultural resonance among Muslims, at least in the abstract. Note how visibly the office has been politically exploited by the "Islamic State" to draw the attention of Muslims.

A fourth issue with which Islamist parties and movements struggle relates to the complex relationship between Islam, the state, and nationalism. Islam is quite clear about its negative views of tribalism, nationalism, or any other cohesive identity that might overshadow Islamic solidarity—at least in principle. The totality of the world Muslim community, the *umma*, represents the ultimate ideal to which Muslims should aspire. Anything that weakens, dilutes, or divides Muslim unity—ethnicity, tribes, states, clans, languages—is undesirable, at least in principle.

Still, the reality of human history is that warring states have always existed, before Islam and during the Islamic era, regardless of religion. What is the basis of that conflict? To put it another way, should nationalism always be viewed as a negative characteristic in Islam? Is it negative, when nationalism is turned against non-Muslim enemies (such as US occupational forces in Iraq since 2003), for example, or where it functions in support of a Muslim population against a non-Muslim force? And what happens when Muslim states are at war with each other? Certainly the state-supported *'ulama* (clerics) have readily found reason why their own state is more Islamically or ideologically just than the enemy state. Yet the contradiction between Islamic unity and local nationalism remains. Indeed, if Islamic unity is the indisputable ideal, there should not even exist an array of separate and distinct "Islamic states"; nonetheless separate states remain the reality. Many of the *'ulama* in India, for instance, opposed the creation of a separate Muslim breakaway state of Pakistan in 1947, precisely because it weakened Muslim unity, even if Pakistan could be an essentially "all-Muslim" state.

The tension between Islam and nationalism will never disappear, especially in the face of Muslim aspiration to greater unity. What, for example, should Muslims make of the phenomenon of Arab nationalism, or pan-Arabism? Many Arabs have instinctively felt that pan-Arabism is a desirable goal, the unity of all Arabic-speaking peoples, from Iraq to Morocco. Indeed, from an Islamic point of view, it does represent a "higher" ideal than mere local state nationalism. Yet Islamic movements have tended to view pan-Arabism negatively. Here the struggle was not usually a theoretical one about Islam versus nationalism, as much as it was shaped by the hostile attitude of Arab nationalist regimes towards Islamist movements that they viewed as rivals or a threat. In reality, then, political tensions—struggles over power—have been great between Islamists and Arab nationalists over much of the modern period. Indeed, Arab nationalists (or any nationalists) tend to be more "secular" in character than Islamist movements, although there is no absolute ideological need to exclude Islam as a cultural value for Arab nationalists.

From a Western perspective Arab nationalism (much less concepts of Islamic solidarity) has been viewed in largely negative terms for two reasons. One is an instinctive Western fear of the emergence of stronger power blocs in the Muslim world, which could challenge or hinder Western geopolitical ambitions for control. Second, such Islamist or even Arab nationalist state attempts have generally failed—even while creating much temporary regional sympathy—due to political inexperience and bad governance. This poor experience in governance by Arab nationalists is due more to the lack of political experience across the region as a whole (partly a product of colonial domination for long periods) than it is determined by the guiding ideology itself.

Even so, there is something of a contradiction here. At a time when Europe is striving towards regional unity in the form of the EU (a higher level of organization than the nation-state), the West has opposed and mocked any Arab or Muslim attempts to achieve the same. Islamists will continue to face the problem of the "illegitimacy" of the Muslim "nation-state" against the aspirational goal of a united umma. Yet how can the West keep peddling the tired European nation-state model (and source of violent European wars) as an alternative to multi-ethnic and multi-religious Muslim states at this point? Surely Muslim aspirations towards greater political unity should be equally viewed as an inherently positive goal, rather than an undesirable one.

Fifth, Islamist movements generally take the lead in fighting Western domination—military, political, cultural—in the Muslim world. They are not alone in this regard: Nationalism in Muslim countries has always resisted foreign power and domination, as we see in the history of innumerable Muslim countries from Algeria to Indonesia. Islamists share this anti-imperial goal no less enthusiastically than (secular) nationalist movements in the region.

In the Islamist struggle against Western colonialism (or Chinese or Russian colonialism) some movements—such as al-Qa'ida and, later, the "Islamic

State" (Da'ish)—have taken the struggle one critical step further by opting to carry the armed struggle into the Western homelands themselves. In doing so these movements of course instantly qualify as "terrorist" in the West, crossing a threshold that even local resistance to Western occupying forces has not done.

Sixth, Islamist movements over a century have increasingly been coming to terms with the challenge from democracy as a governing principle or ideology. Here contradictions abound, however, as we will discuss in greater detail below. If the basis of Shari'a is fundamentally divine (to the extent it derives from revelation), then codified law derived from the Shari'a (fiqh) cannot be reduced to the outcome of human debate and legislation. Legislators in an Islamic state cannot simply decide that it is "permissible" to sell or consume alcohol—or, similarly, to permit the use of interest. In this case, "Man" does not have the right to overturn "God's laws." Thus Islamic democracies (or partial democracies like Iran or Pakistan) have established High Shari'a Councils or courts that in effect pass on the Islamic legitimacy of a given piece of parliamentary legislation. (In principle this resembles the institution, say, of the US Supreme Court, which passes on the constitutionality of legislation from the US Congress, although religion is not supposed to figure in such decisions—even though it might influence the decisions of individual justices.)

Even where Islamists sometimes feel uncomfortable with granting too much authority to the electorate or to an elected legislature, many of them comment on one obvious benefit of a democratic system: The people can actually get rid of a ruler who is no longer wanted. Islam may teach that rulers, to be legitimate, must be "just" and consult with the people (among other qualifications), yet there are no provisions for removing the unjust ruler. Indeed, 'ulama who in principle might be qualified to pass on the Islamic legitimacy of a ruler or his policies at any time in history, might find it dangerous to their health to declare a ruler "un-Islamic" and worthy of overthrow.

In practice, then, Islamists have increasingly come to accept many of the basic principles of democracy as desirable in Islamic states, although the devil is in the details, of course. Movements like the Muslim Brotherhood have long been active in trade union politics and elections, as well as in other professional organizations. They have often gone beyond that involvement to participate in legislative politics in Egypt, Palestine (Hamas), Jordan, Yemen, Iraq, Tunisia (Ennahda), Morocco, Algeria, Pakistan, and elsewhere. Salafi movements have long reviled democracy and elections as un-Islamic and a Western innovation, yet they changed their tune in Egypt in 2012, for example. When it became obvious, that is, that national elections would be the new forum in which a new national struggle for power would be enacted, they thereupon decided to participate in elections. The same happened in Pakistan. When democracy becomes a key channel to power, most Islamists end up choosing to participate. The lessons gained from that experience alone are invaluable and key to arguments about processes of evolution within political Islam.

As Islamist (or, less ideologically, *Islamic*) movements become an inevitable part of the Muslim political scene, we witness the emergence of ever less violent, even forward-looking movements on the Islamic political spectrum. Since 2003 the ruling Justice and Progress Party (AKP) in Turkey has been highly effective and quite remarkable in its accomplishments in its first decade—arguably the most effective in modern Turkish democratic history. That progress came about despite the current major mistakes the AKP has made since 2013, when after ten years it has grown corrupt and its leader has adopted a markedly authoritarian style (even though still elected to office). In addition, the Hizmet (Service) movement in Turkey (not a political party), founded by Fethullah Gülen, is a remarkable civil Islamic movement—one of the largest, most progressive, and tolerant movements anywhere in the Muslim world. It emphasizes religious tolerance, inter-civilizational dialog, and the overwhelming need for modern scientific education—more schools rather than more mosques to best serve the Muslim world.

The Role of Power Relationships in Advocacy of Shari'a

There are at least two distinct dynamics of political Islam (and advocacy of Shari'a): Islamist parties *out of power*, who seek participation in the system (power); and Islamist parties *in power*, who want to retain power. Such dynamics are common to all political systems and hardly unique to Islamist parties, but Islamist parties bring special ideological considerations to bear.

The question of Shari'a and its place in governance is heavily influenced by the power dynamic involved: Are Islamists seeking to gain entry into the system (power), or to maintain power (their position in the system)? Islamists out of power brandish Shari'a and the Islamic agenda as a weapon against entrenched authoritarian regimes, which the Islamists charge with being non-Islamic, that is, illegitimate. How does an entrenched regime fight against the charge of being non-Islamic, except by challenging or eliminating the Islamists leveling the charge? Yet harsh treatment of the Islamic opposition can be dangerous when the regime's very legitimacy is in question in the minds of the public, who might then lend street support to the Islamic challengers (as happened during the Arab Spring in Tunisia, Egypt, Libya, and Syria).

Power and Change in Government
In the West we routinely place much emphasis upon the rule of law and the need to follow constitutional procedure in any change of government. In societies and polities with relatively new and fragile governing procedures, however, the issue of the rule of law is not as simple as its mere evocation would seem. *Whose* rule of law? And the rule of *whose* law? How were the rules of the game established? By whom, and with whose interests at stake? What if the rules of the game seem to be unfair and disadvantage any new contenders for power? How can or should the rules of the game be changed? All these questions pose issues that are a recipe for instability and for the potential use of violence in changing the system—especially when the system may indeed not be "fair" or provide a level playing field for other players. Glib Western references to "rule of law," then, often miss the point.

Such was the case with the government of Muhammad al-Morsi, elected in 2012 in the first presidential elections in the history of Egypt. A broad variety of differing judgments concerning the character of his year in office exist. Yet it is not simply a question of assessing his rule—his legitimately elected government was overthrown by a military coup one year later—but the *conditions* under which his rule took place. The constitution was still in the process of being written; the *rules of the game themselves* were under contention. So simple appeal to "rule of law" provides very little answer to these questions. Each side sought to write a constitution and create rules of the game that inevitably favored their own party. How do power relations change, or are they changed, under such circumstances? Power, often raw power, determines these questions of "rule of law." Who controls the ministries of power: military, intelligence, security, police? (Morsi, even as president, did not). Moreover, how are the rules applied, and in support of whose interests? If there are rules, who will enforce the rules, and how?

In examining the major cases of when Islamist parties have come to power in the Middle East over the past few decades, this precise question immediately emerges: How did they come to power? At least six of the following quite diverse cases with Islamist movements have gone on to establish an "Islamic State."

- The Saudi State: The present Kingdom of Saudi Arabia has of course been in existence for over a century. It does not officially designate itself as an Islamic State, but does claim that its sole constitution is the Qur'an. It applies Shari'a law fairly strictly in accordance with an ultra-conservative school of Wahhabism, or Salafism. It came to power via an armed mujahidin movement that conquered the central region and, through political alliances, spread its conquests across the country and beyond. Still, this case is not, properly speaking, an example of modern Islamism, although the Saudi state is undeniably a form of "Islamic State."

- The Iranian Revolution of 1979 came to power amidst a genuine *social revolution and drawn-out civil chaos*, involving multiple parties across a political spectrum that contested for power—royalists, socialists, communists, nationalists, and Islamists. In the end, the Islamists outmaneuvered all their opponents and gained power, notably the more hard-line Islamist faction dominated by Ayatollah Khomeini. Here the Islamists achieved power through manipulation of a chaotic political scene in a revolutionary context. The Khomeini government maintained a uniquely *revolutionary* interpretation of (Shi'ite) Islam.

- Sudan: Sudanese Islamists came to power in 1989 via a *bloodless military coup* backed by a group that would call itself The National Islamic Front. This Front is the ruling party in what is essentially a one-party state—the Republic of Sudan. Although Sudan does not officially declare itself an Islamic State, it has declared that Shari'a is the foundation of national law, and it applies it in varying ways. Prominent Islamists have played major roles in all levels of state politics.

- Afghanistan: The Taliban came to power in 1996 by *military means in a civil war*. They crushed other Islamist movements and militias that had nearly destroyed the country in a previous eight-year civil war among Islamist militias. The Taliban brought peace and order, declared the Islamic Emirate of Afghanistan and imposed strict Shari'a law, until the regime was overthrown by US forces in 2001.

- Turkey: The AKP (Justice and Development Party)—the current ruling party (as of 2016)—represents a highly moderate Islamist party even though it does not designate itself as such. Rather, it declares itself to be a socially conservative democratic party. The party itself disavows any Islamist label (partly due to Turkish constitutional prohibitions) but emerges from a long succession of variously suppressed Islamist/Islamic parties over the past several decades. It achieved power through honest *democratic elections* and went on to win three successive, fair national elections. It is the first Islamic party to achieve national power by democratic means in the Muslim world. Regrettably, its leader, Recep Tayyip Erdoğan, has in recent times come to abuse the structures of democracy and to harass and persecute his enemies, but he has technically not yet stepped outside of the democratic framework of elected leader.

- Pakistan: Pakistan's politics have always been deeply imbued with Islam; indeed Islam is the very founding principle and raison d'être for the existence of the country. Islamist policies reached a high point primarily in the 1980s under the military leader General Zia ul-Haq, who *imposed* a broad program of what he called Islamization, with heavy emphasis on Shari'a. Pakistan's domestic politics are some of the most Islamist-oriented in the whole Muslim world, under both military rulers as well as civilian elected leaders.

- Egypt: The Muslim Brotherhood came to power in *legitimate elections* in 2012 and was overthrown the next year by military coup. It was still in the process of formulating its basic policies when it was overthrown.

- "Islamic State" (ISIS, ISIL, *Da'ish*) was officially formed under that name in Iraq in 1996 as a resistance movement to US occupation but achieved prominence through the *military conquest* of significant territory and imposition of administrative rule over it in 2014. It also declared itself a Caliphate. It declares full Shari'a law and has been highly rigid, indeed brutal in its literal interpretation of Shari'a, including a promotion of a number of obscure Islamic doctrines and practices not normally acknowledged by most Islamists and often taken out of context. Both the West and regional forces seek its overthrow by military means.

We thus have a variety of Islamist/Islamic states coming to power by various means. Other than Turkey and its special conditions, Islamists might well ask the question as to whether they will ever be permitted by the domestic or international order to come to power. Can they have any faith in non-violent means? If the answer appears to be no, immediate implications arise: Will Islamists instead then seek to come to power by force or revolution? The answer to this question also has great implications for the application of Shari'a law, however interpreted.

We can see, therefore, how power relations are central to the entire question of how the Islamic state in general will be conceived, what its characteristics will be, and how power relations will affect it both inside and outside the system.

PART TWO: QUESTIONS OF IDENTITY AND TRUST IN ISLAMIC GOVERNANCE

Identity may be the single most important factor in examining Middle East politics today, transcending in importance perhaps even theology or Islamic law/Shari'a. How is this so?

This issue of identity leads directly into the question of *trust in institutions*, a vital factor in the development of stable, recognized governing authorities and cohesive societies. It also affects the distribution of power and the place for Islamists within that order. Rule of law can have no place if there is no trust of institutions, and especially in institutions of state. Who trusts institutions? The first question anyone asks is, who controls the institutions?

Whom do they represent? The answer reflects directly on the central question of identity.

In examining any state a key question to ask is, what is the *basic unit of belonging* in the state? Do people feel they belong to—or owe loyalty to—a *national* unit that defines their identity and forms the borders within which they live and work? Or is it a racial or ethnic community that commands their first loyalty? Does the state represent primarily one *dominant group* that holds sway over other groups, or is their some belief that the state tends to represent everyone? Is the primary level of identity and loyalty regional, linguistic or ethnic, or religious? Is the power of that dominant group considered basically acceptable, or not?

Objective conditions, too, affect issues of personal and group identity. We all have multiple identities: religious, sectarian, ethnic, linguistic, regional, political, economic (class), gender, professional, even personal interests or hobbies that characterize us. Or are we a global citizen? Among all these identities, which identity is dominant? The salience of any one element of identity over another is obviously highly situational, depending upon a variety of circumstances of time, place, and situation.

Personal identity within the context of the state and society is to a considerable extent *situationally* determined. First, while I may have my own self-selected identity, do you acknowledge that identity, or do you accord me another one? If I say I am Iraqi, you can say I am Iraqi Shi'a, hence not part of the (formerly) dominant Iraqi Sunni identity. I thus lose a degree of control over my self-chosen identity. Others may deprive me of my chosen identity.

For instance, a Jew living in Germany in the post-World War I environment of the liberal democratic Weimar Republic around 1922, if asked his identity, might respond: "European, German, Jewish, male, professor of sociology, from Bavaria (Southern Germany), socialist, an amateur cyclist." Fifteen years later, as Hitler began to impose the power of the Nazi Party in Germany, that same professor, if asked his identity, would have only one that meant anything to the state or society: Jewish. No other identity would matter and that identity would be a question of life or death.

Alternatively, an Iraqi woman under Saddam Hussein's secular dictatorship in the 1990s might be Arab, Iraqi, from the south, an artist, Shi'ite. After the US overthrow of Saddam and his Sunni-based regime in 2003 and the sudden ascension of Shi'ites to power in Iraq, that Shi'ite identity would suddenly become central to one's relative position of power within society, as well as a vital aspect of personal security depending on the neighborhood in which she lived. This situation of community is also heard from a Lebanese Christian writer, once commenting that he was "Arab, Christian, and culturally Muslim." In other words, the Muslim world is his ambient culture.

It is conditions of chaos and disorder that most quickly and deeply reveal basic, gut identity. These are the conditions when my very safety and welfare are at stake. What ties will be the ones most likely to provide me with the greatest degree of safety and welfare? In much of the world it is subnational ties that will provide the greatest security: the tribe, ethnic group, religious ties, sectarian ties, regional ties, clan ties—these all start figuring more importantly than institutions. Where do you go and to whom do you turn for protection, food, shelter, solidarity, with no questions asked? These are in reality the conditions of a great part of the Middle East, especially when the region is in chaos. Yet this reduction of identity to its most basic components also results in a shattered social order in which there is no trust in any institutions, only in personal ties. If you are a Sunni having trouble in the neighborhood, do you go to a local magistrate if that magistrate is Shi'ite?

Such sectarian questions, for example, now matter more in Iraq than institutional ones. The key issue then becomes: How can the state build confidence in its neutrality and evenhandedness so that citizens will rely on institutions to provide justice and security more than upon personal connections? This predicament is true in most of the developing world, but even beyond. Do African-Americans in some parts of the US, for example, trust their local police or legal system for equitable treatment? Do Algerians in Paris have confidence in the local security forces? Trust in specific institutions becomes a fundamental touchstone in determining which identity is the most prominent one for me. When conditions are safer, when we have greater trust in the neutrality of institutions, we will then all struggle to attain broader and more universal identities as nationals of a state, or even as human beings calling for equal rights globally.

For Muslims, one key level of identity (but not the only one) is Muslim—at least vis-à-vis other religious groups. At this level Shari'a matters very much as a symbol of Muslim identity. What good is belief in Shari'a, though, when Shi'a are killing Sunni or vice versa, or when Sunni Turks are killing Sunni Kurds? Shari'a may not be of much help in the case of fractured Muslim identities. Moreover, it may be a barrier of discrimination when a state claims it seeks to reach out above Islam to establish an all-inclusive national identity.

The problem facing all states and societies is, then, what basis of identity is the most ideal—for the individual, the state, and the world? Among the multiple identities of any individual, which combination is it that empowers an individual to lead a successful life? Or enables a state to function well with the participation of all its citizens in its benefits? Or allows for a national identity that does not threaten war with other national identities? What is the role of governance in helping determine these things? And what, then, is the place of Shari'a in terms of religious life and individual participation in society and the state?

It has been said that politics and governance are about who gets what, when, and how. How does Shari'a fit into this equation? And how do relationships of power—and the rules of power—affect these issues?

Dilemmas of Contemporary Islamist Political Thinking
Islamists face a variety of dilemmas in thinking about the place of Shari'a in politics and governance.

First, should Islamists enter politics at all? Is it better first to devote attention to *da'wa*—the propagation of "correct" Islam among other Muslims? Such preaching would represent a bottom-up approach; it implies education and consciousness-raising, preparing the mentality of the public as the necessary prerequisite to establishing a Shari'a-based political and social order. (It is important to note here that most Islamists have little interest in converting non-Muslims to Islam; their major task is to bring uncommitted Muslims to the "correct" path of thinking and commitment to their religion.)

Alternatively, Islamists can adopt a top-down approach to the implementation of Shari'a and the creation of an Islamic state. Top-down of course implies a degree of *imposition* of values, running the risk of adopting an authoritarian order, and abandoning more democratic mechanisms. Given the long tradition of authoritarian rule in the Middle East, an authoritarian approach sadly may represent the most common political environment in which Shari'a law might be applied.

Islamists then face the question of *how* to come to power. Do they enjoy sufficient backing of the public that they would stand a chance in democratic elections? In most Muslim countries Islamists have gained a positive reputation for struggling over the years against illegitimate, non-Islamic, incompetent, or authoritarian rule. They have been silenced, jailed, tortured, or killed in their campaigns against existing regimes. Thus when the first free elections are held in almost any country, Islamists tend to win. This reality has been a powerful factor in actually predisposing Islamists towards adopting some sort of democratic order. What happens, though, when they lose popular support?

Indeed, as Islamist parties become barred from politics, or removed by military force from office as in Egypt in 2013, the legitimate question arises as to whether they will ever be allowed to participate in the political order. In that case, if the answer seems to be no, perhaps political violence remains their only other alternative.

Still, the true test of Islamist political skill is revealed not in initial, but in subsequent elections. Islamists elected for the first time to office are required to demonstrate the capabilities of their leadership and policies in managing the multiple problems their societies face. Indeed Islamists may often lack technocratic experience due to long exclusion from the governing process in an earlier era. Yet once in power, Islamists must deliver. If they do not, they run the risk of being voted out of office in the second round.

Losing power in a subsequent election also poses a new ideological dilemma. Should an Islamic party devoted to implementation of God's law *be allowed* to be defeated? The names of Islamist parties come into play here as well. The main Shi'ite political party in Lebanon calls itself *Hizballah*, "the party of God." Can a "party of God" be unelected? And what then are the other parties, if not of God? Actually in most Muslim countries, such as Turkey, the Islamic party has adopted a non-religious name—AKP, or Party of Justice and Progress; or in Morocco, 'Adl wa'l Ihsan (Justice and Welfare); or the Muslim Brotherhood in Yemen, Hizb al-Islah (Party of Reform). These names are more in accord with existing contemporary politics and help remove any suggestion that Islamist parties have an inside track to God.

Even so, should the fate of this huge religious and social project of the Islamists have to depend upon the whims of the electorate? Or should Islamists adopt methods whereby they remain in power anyway, contrary to electoral results? The leading Tunisian Islamist thinker and politician Shaykh Rashid al-Ghannushi commented that if Islamist parties fail to win and maintain public electoral support, the fault lies with the party, not with the people; the party must then go back to the drawing board and come up with better and more persuasive ideas. His view represents an idealistic response, of course; the exigencies of politics make it hard for any political party to give up power readily, unless the democratic order is well established.

Islamists often brandish the slogan al-Islam, huwwa al-hall—Islam is the solution. One could even be willing to accept this proposition in principle. Nonetheless, the immediate response is to say Islam may have the solutions, but at the same time ask: What are the specifics of the party's platform on education, the economy, foreign policy, trade, the legal and political system? Then we can determine whether an Islam-inspired agenda may or may not have what it takes to rule effectively. Shari'a offers no clear guidelines of rule or policies whatsoever. It may offer inspirational principles, but it is the specifics of governance that matter in the end.

Islamists also need to decide what the limits are of an elected legislature to pass laws that might be seen to contravene some interpretations of Shari'a. In principle such a situation would not be permitted; such laws would be struck down by a High Shari'a Court, much as a Supreme Court in other countries might rule on the constitutionality of legislative bills. Yet the dilemma remains: How far are human legislatures empowered to pass laws that touch upon certain concepts of Shari'a, or on the method of its implementation? (Force, violence, arrest?) This question is actually a profound dilemma for all ideological regimes, whether secular or religious. To the true believer, if the ideology demands certain policy actions or certain structures of rule, then it does not matter whether people want it, like it, or support it. In a religious context, radical jihadis such as ISIS can claim that the order they are imposing is God's order, and that what the citizenry thinks about it is irrelevant. People must behave according to such God-given dictates; no further justification is needed, nor are elections or public opinion remotely relevant to the process.

There are at least two good reasons why such an approach cannot work, however. First, the Qur'an itself states that "Allah intends for you ease, and does not want to make things difficult for you" [2:185]; and "Allah does not want to place you in difficulty" [5:6]. The implication is that the practice of religion should bring ease and not hardship. Second, there is the well-known Quranic statement "There is no compulsion in religion" (2.256). Both of these verses are of course subject to interpretation, but it is extremely difficult to justify the kind of compulsion and brutality behind, for example, ISIS' interpretation of the Islamic way of life. Finally, from a practical perspective, people will not willingly support a regime that delivers death, suffering, and hardship in the name of Islam; indeed that is not the way most Muslims interpret their faith. In the end we are drawn into questions of popular will, popular desires, and democratic practice, which do indeed present contradictions. Even democracies are limited by the realities of existing conditions.

Islamists also debate the degree to which Islamist governance should impose morality. All states impose morality to one extent or another. No state will condone murder or theft, crimes which were originally included within the Ten Commandments in the Western tradition. In Turkey an Islamist once mentioned to me that, after watching countries like Saudi Arabia impose morality, including obligatory prayers and clothing codes, Turkish Islamists were debating how far the state should go in this direction. "Perhaps the Gates of Hell must remain open; the State cannot prohibit entry." In other words, in certain realms of morality, some of these questions become an issue to be resolved between the individual and God, and not by the State.

Indeed, there is great variation from state to state among laws passed and imposed. The US passed laws in the 1920s banning alcohol that lasted thirteen years. Should abortion be legal or illegal? What about drugs, and what kinds? Sexual freedoms? Even the West limits some sexual freedoms in banning sex with minor children, though the exact age of consent varies widely. The range of moral issues is broad and involves rights of the individual as well as protection of society. Islamists, too, face these problems of how and where to legislate morality and how to punish transgressions. The Saudi answer, say, to five daily prayers is to impose them. Yet what virtue does the individual gain in the eyes of God for doing the right thing out of compulsion? Implementation of Shari'a becomes quite complex in this realm and, again, there is no consensus in its interpretation.

The Turkish moderate Islamist party now in power, the AKP, at one point debated the issue of whether or not to criminalize marital infidelity. Liberals everywhere were horrified. The penalty possibly to be imposed was actually just a fine. The issue was raised not just as a moral, but also as a social concern. Just as drugs and alcohol create huge social dislocations, so do broken families. If the law complicates casual marital infidelity and the damage it causes to the family structure (their argument ran), then that is in the greater social interest. The argument is intriguing, but in the end the issue was dropped.

Ultimately, despite all the public controversy over morality and punishments, public opinion polls seem to indicate that most Muslims are far more concerned about the quality of life and governance than they are about moral issues relating to Shari'a. In principle Shari'a law is viewed as a positive virtue, but questions of employment, welfare, medical facilities, education, personal freedoms, and the right to speak out rate more highly than questions of Islamic legitimacy as perceived by the 'ulama (clerics).

Islamists who have an interest in governing will have to learn to excel in the arts of management and governance if they wish to remain elected; piety is simply not enough. Indeed, one of the primary reasons for the success of the Turkish AKP was that it excelled in managing municipalities: garbage was collected, bureaucrats were responsive, life improved. These material and practical issues are the criteria in most societies for good governance rather than moral posturing. Yet, even in US politics, moral issues or moral posturing do play significant roles in presidential campaigns, though not as much as do pocketbook issues.

Shaykh Rashid al-Ghannushi in Tunisia also once remarked that it would be a tragedy if Islamists came to power, imposed Islamic values, failed to rule competently, and the people ultimately ended up "hating" Islam. One wonders whether aspects of this concern do not apply to Saudi Arabia or Iran in certain areas as well.

Preservation of ideological purity too, remains a concern in many Islamist movements. To what extent does mere entry into politics corrupt the purity of their vision, or compel compromise? Should Islamists join in coalitions with other parties whose overall goals may be antithetical to Islamists, such as a socialist or communist party, even where transient tactical agreement might exist on a specific issue? Here, then, the realm of *compromise* thus enters into the equation; yet this is probably a valuable experience for Islamists who wish to participate in politics but must do so on a realistic basis.

Proclamation of an Islamic state raises further issues about the *role of clerics* in politics. Interestingly, the majority of Islamist leaders are not clerics or students of Islamic theology. They tend to be engineers, doctors, or technicians of various kinds. This in itself is an interesting phenomenon since it suggests that when an individual has had only limited exposure to the humanities—philosophy, psychology, sociology, political science—he tends to adopt a "systems approach" to governance: All it takes is a good blueprint—a divinely-inspired set of rules—in order to implement the good society, and the rest will take care of itself. A strictly technical education might make less allowance for human foibles and drives that constitute the really complicating factors in any political system. In short, even if one talks about Shari'a, more questions about *implementation* arise than are solved by the concept. Human, administrative, and managerial skills and experience are required in any system to make it work.

Should clerics then provide leadership in Islamist states? In most Sunni Islamist states they have not. The "Islamic State" or ISIS is quite conspicuous in its leadership by a man who possesses serious theological credentials and proclaims himself a Caliph. Mullah Omar, former leader of the Taliban, was also a prominent cleric. Yet Sunni states have historically—while usually led by leaders of "secular" background (tribal or military)—also maintained a body of 'ulama or Islamic scholars whose duty it was to advise on religious questions and provide religious legitimacy to the leadership. Not surprisingly, it was easy for such state-owned 'ulama to be corrupted or suborned by power, as well as discouraged from criticizing the leader who fed them.

Shi'ite tradition foresaw this dilemma early on, since the earliest experience of Shi'a with Sunni power centers was a negative one; they watched the descendants of the Prophet sidelined from the office of the Caliphate as a result of politics and power. Shi'ite religious tradition thus has suspicions about the corrupting character of power. The Shi'ite "quietist tradition" among many Ayatollahs preferred clerics to remain outside the power structure, to avoid involvement in day-to-day politics and administration, and to only speak out on major issues of governance in general terms on critical issues in order to help keep the political process on a wise track. Ironically it was Grand Ayatollah Khomeini, the leading figure in the foundation of the Islamic Republic of Iran in 1979, who advocated the revolutionary thesis within Shi'ite theology of *Velayat-e-Faqih* or "Rule of the Jurisprudent." Turning traditional Shi'ite jurisprudence on its head, the clergy under this system came to dominate the political order in Iran. Indeed, just as the tradition had feared, it quickly led to the corruption of the clerics through proximity to power and involvement in its everyday affairs.

As a consequence, Islamists are still left with the question of the role of clerics or jurisprudents within the Islamic state. Some clerics indeed might also happen to make good politicians or administrators, but in principle their training makes it less likely. The practical day-to-day elements of good governance and policy-making are in no way guaranteed simply because of accepting Shari'a law as such—its guidance is far too generalized. In fact, the reality is that governance in the Muslim world has shown no signs of improvement even as clerics grew more deeply involved in politics or sought to apply Shari'a more intensely. It seems that Shari'a, while providing a moral framework, is not in itself is enough to guarantee good governance.

Most of this discussion has been about theory in the interpretation and practice of Islam. In the end, though, does Islam itself really matter in this discussion of governance, power, and ideology? A good case can be made that power struggles and communal conflict are a given in all human politics; we do not need the explanatory power of Islam to elucidate them. As a matter of fact, most of these same questions and dilemmas would exist in governance without Islam. (I elaborate on these arguments in considerable detail, both historical and present, in my book A World Without Islam [Little Brown, 2011].) Islam in that case can be seen as simply providing a banner, an ideology behind which power relationships contend. In this context, Islam primarily serves to lend cultural flavor and character to broader, more universal human issues.

As a result, if Islam were excluded from the picture, would not conflicting communities find other grounds for strife? The Shi'a-Sunni conflict, for example, has deep roots in power relationships and regional power struggles; it even carries ethnic overtones of Arab versus Persian. Reformers who struggle against authoritarian rule in the Middle East would not require specifically Islamic justifications by which to condemn existing regimes; ideological arguments always abound. From this perspective, issues of Shari'a might perhaps be considered as little more than the turf or the cultural framework within which power groups contend, using religious arguments to justify their cause.

How much, perhaps, is the debate over Shari'a law and secular law simply an empty argument over the longer term, especially when it can be argued that neither of these systems in themselves is guaranteed to deliver good governance? In fact, the increasing participation of Islam in the political order has forced a rapid evolution of political thinking within it. When Islamism is out of power, it actually enjoys a certain luxury. It can argue indefinitely about theology, Shari'a, what is legal and what is not, or whether democracy and parliaments are compatible with Islam. As Islam enters the political realm, however, the pressures to adapt to the multiple realities of contemporary political life force an accelerated evolution in Islamic political thinking. Islamic thinking becomes forced into more nuanced considerations, much more so than if it had simply focused upon the realm of traditional family law. We see examples of this change in the surprising willingness of Egyptian Salafis to enter the election process in 2011, which they had once condemned as non-Islamic: They realized that the democratic process was going to adjudicate power relationships into the future and that if they did not participate, they would find themselves losing out in that arena.

Objective conditions also exert major impact in determining the degree of radicalism or violence that is introduced into political Islam. There can be no doubt that the American "Global War on Terror" (with its destruction of the Afghan and Iraqi states) and the deep conflict within Somalia and Yemen (even prior to the Arab Spring) have stirred up violent local opposition to US warfare, with its use of drones, proxy forces (Ethiopians in Somalia), and US occupation of those countries—all this had a massive radicalizing impact upon Salafi and jihadi groups in the region. Extreme political violence imposed on these countries has created major social turmoil, displacement of local populations, and the creation of a flow of refugees both internal and external. The resulting chaos inflamed populations and offered openings to radical militia that would otherwise not have been possible. In this way, doctrine is deeply affected by objective circumstances unrelated specifically to Islam.

Finally, under conditions of chaos (*fawdha*) there is a tendency for people to retreat to core minimalist goals in which sheer survival becomes the top priority. As the 14th-century Islamic scholar in Syria, Ibn Taymiyya, observed, chaos is worse than oppressive rule—a profoundly conservative doctrine, reflected also in the thinking of Thomas Hobbes some two centuries later. Chaos and the struggle for survival do not offer conditions conducive to creative thinking in politics or to liberal interpretation of religion; communities instead hunker down and cling to basics, asserting their identity. This reaction is perfectly exemplified by the Chechens in 2000 who, during the savage Russian destruction of all of Grozny, embraced full Shari'a law including the classical physical punishments (*hudud*) as an act of cultural-religious defiance against their non-Muslim Russian oppressors.

Innovative thought in the interpretation of Islam and Shari'a in governance is therefore not likely to emerge under the present conditions of most of the Middle East. Turkey and Iran are the two leading candidates for providing contemporary interpretations of Islam. Even so, Islam will never be absent from the political arena in the Muslim world, regardless of the degree to which secular thinking also spreads within Islamic societies. It will always provide a political vocabulary and cultural framework in political thought, just as Confucianism will always be a part of Chinese political thinking. And Muslims in the West possess the unique opportunity of having the security and freedom to contribute heavily to the process of new thinking in Muslims' understanding of their own religion.

Perspectives on the Sunni-Shi'ite Sectarian Conflict

Some degree of rivalry has always existed between Shi'a and Sunnis in Islam. The conflict waxes and wanes. Over history, however, coexistence rather than conflict has been much more the rule.

Nevertheless, this century seems to have ushered in a renewed and virulent phase of Sunni-Shi'ite conflict. While the causes are multiple, the new outbreak was most immediately sparked by the US invasion of Iraq in 2003, which precipitated a sea change in the balance between Sunni and Shi'ite power in the eastern Arab world. Iraqi Arab Sunnis, who had long constituted the ruling minority within the state, lost control of the state with the overthrow of Saddam Hussein's Ba'th regime. Shortly thereafter the Iraqi Shi'a gained dominance over the new Iraqi government through new and free elections that reflected their majority status in the country. The repercussions of this power reversal across the region were powerful and are still far from over. Forces unleashed by the Arab Spring starting in 2011 further exacerbated this new sectarian confrontation.

Yet the actual character of this sectarian conflict is mostly not about Sunni and Shi'ite theology. We need to explore the roots of this old split in the Muslim world in order to understand how they affect present circumstances—which currently have culminated in a major anti-Iran, anti-Shi'ite campaign most directly by Saudi Arabia. This confrontation is driven by far more than religious issues.

First, a few basic facts: The Shi'a today make up perhaps some 13 percent of all Muslims worldwide. They tend to be concentrated in a population belt stretching from Syria, Iraq, the Persian Gulf, Iran, Afghanistan, Pakistan, and India (where Shi'a make up as much as 25 to 30 percent of the overall Muslim population).

ORIGINS OF THE CONFLICT

The actual origin of the conflict is straightforward: It stems from a factional struggle between two groups over succession to the leadership of the new Muslim community after the death of the Prophet Muhammad in 632 CE. This successor (Caliph, or *Khalifa* in Arabic) would represent the political leadership of the new community, but would have no prophetic function. As the first, victorious group, the Sunnis advocated the *selection* of a successor from among leading notables of the Muslim community. These notables included heavy representation from the dominant Quraysh tribe that, at an earlier juncture, had actually perceived the Prophet's mission as a threat to their authority and had fought the new Muslim community. The second group advocated transmission of the leadership via the Prophet's *bloodline*, in this case, to 'Ali, an early convert, close confidant and the Prophet's son-in-law. This group was known as the "partisans" (*shi'a*) of 'Ali.

'Ali was passed over three times in favor of non-bloodline Caliphs but was finally selected as the fourth Caliph. With the eventual assassination of 'Ali, however, leadership of the new Muslim community came quickly to be dominated by Sunnis who held military power. In a traumatic and fateful moment the grandson of 'Ali was "martyred" in a military battle over leadership of the community—an event forever commemorated across the Shi'ite world in the annual mass grieving ceremonies during the month of 'Ashura. (Such power struggles over religious authority are of course well known in the annals of the bloody conflict over control of the Papacy in the Christian tradition, too.)

Once the Muslim community had split and blood had been shed over the succession issue, the two communities began to diverge over time; each community—as communities tend to do—gradually took on specific characteristics: lore, tradition, literature, myths, community rituals, and celebrations. Thus the original issue of succession to the Prophet was no longer a live question, but evolved into a rivalry between *communities*. (We can likewise see this in Western history with the evolution of distinctive, rival Catholic and Protestant communities—at odds more over questions of power and authority than over theology.) Both Muslim communities worshipped the same God, shared the same Qur'an, and large numbers of the same traditions of the words and deeds of the Prophet (*Hadith*). The Shi'a, however, additionally venerated 'Ali, an act which, according to strict Sunni interpretation, was blasphemous; many Shi'a were believed to curse the earliest Caliphs, especially 'Umar, for his early opposition to the Prophet before the new Muslim community was formed. The Shi'a additionally venerated a tradition of successor Imams from the bloodline of the Prophet through 'Ali, and even developed a mystical view of the lives of these successors and their transcendent spiritual roles. There were up to eleven such revered "Imams" or successors to 'Ali, representing different schools of theology in Shi'ism. These schools variously venerated either the fifth, seventh, or twelfth Imam (to come); this latter school constitutes the major Shi'ite tradition today (the so-called "Twelvers" in Iran.) There is no strong tradition of conflict among these Shi'ite schools.

Additionally, although 'Ali himself is the founding figure of the Shi'ite tradition, he also happens to be held in deep esteem by many Sunnis, who see him as an early, brave ("lion-hearted"), and loyal follower of the Prophet from the earliest days, a man whose writings and poetry on moral issues is widely regarded. It is not that Sunnis dislike 'Ali; they object to Shi'ite veneration of him which is seen by some as blasphemous, as *shirk*, for any sharing of pure devotion to the one God. (Even the Prophet himself is not to be revered or worshipped in strict Salafi/Wahhabi Islam. There is to be no intermediary in man's relationship with God.) Caliphs in the Sunni tradition have largely been de facto power-holders (sultans, kings, emirs) within the Sunni community and not often so venerated.

The strong Shi'ite reverence for 'Ali is regarded with particular suspicion and hatred by fundamentalist Sunnis (Salafis), who blame the Shi'a for the early and terrible split in the facade of unity of Islam. These Salafis, particularly in the Saudi version of Wahhabism, display an additional hatred for any kind of mysticism or saints, or Sufi (mystical) religious tradition, or miracles. Wahhabis even destroyed the very tomb of the Prophet himself in later centuries lest the Prophet's grave should become a site of pilgrimage, or an object of worship and reverence in its own right.

Questions of ethnicity also crept into the Sunni-Shi'ite schism. In a perhaps strangely contemporary perspective, Islam as a faith has little tolerance for ethnic difference. The Qur'an says "Truly, the noblest of you with God is the most pious." (Quran, 49:13) The Prophet Muhammad is reported to have said: "O people! … An Arab is not better than a non-Arab and a non-Arab is not better than an Arab, and a red (i.e. white tinged with red) person is not better than a black person and a black person is not better than a red person, except in piety."

However, since Islam began in the heart of the Arabian Peninsula, there was a tendency among some early Arab Muslims to assume that—just as the Jews had Judaism as their own religion, making them God's chosen people—Islam was God's religion for the Arabs. Yet orthodox Islam fought this racial concept persistently. Nonetheless, fairly early on with the spread of Islam to Persian-speaking regions, some Arabs assumed they themselves were the "truer" Muslims since the message of Islam had been delivered in Arabic and to an Arab. There was some tendency toward jockeying for power and position in the newly emerging empire on an ethnic basis; Shi'ism, as an alternative community and religious tradition to the Sunni power structure, thus proved attractive to many non-Arabs. These events tended to lend a tinge of ethnicity to matters of religion. The superiority of Arabs as the first Muslims even today remains a subtle prejudice among some Arab Muslims. Islam itself is very clear, however, in rejecting any element of ethnicity or race—in principle—as playing any role in Islam and the Islamic community.

The Shi'ite branch of Islam itself is hardly monolithic; as we noted, there are at least four major schools distinguished primarily by which early Imam (and descendant of the Prophet) they hold as their guide. This includes followers of the fifth Imam (Zaydis or "Fivers"), Isma'ilis (or "Seveners"), and Ja'faris ("Twelvers," the largest single group). Alawites in Syria also represent a heterodox form of Shi'ism. These schools are rarely in serious conflict with one another, though, while anti-Shi'ite pressures from Sunnis also serve to stimulate a greater unity among these Shi'ite schools.

Shi'ism and Power: As with all religions, the power of religious belief as a motivating human force is too important to be ignored by political leaders; they regularly seek to press it into the service of the ruling authority. Because of hostility of the Sunni state—the overwhelmingly dominant force in the first half-century of Islam—Shi'ite political thinking developed an early suspicion of the flawed moral nature of the State that seemed to be driven more by power than religious impulse. Shi'a also recognized the corrupting quality of proximity to power. Whereas Sunni clerics often played a major role in providing the religious support and justification to the actions of rulers, some traditions of Shi'ism instinctively warned clerics away from too close association with power (as state-supported clergy) as a potentially corrupting element. Some Shi'ite clerics often took the position of standing aloof from day-to-day politics of the state, choosing to intervene or speak out on political issues only on the most important of occasions, and only in speaking of general principles. This tradition of political distance came to be known as the "quietist tradition"; in principle it shielded clerics from the corrupting force of power and the state.

In point of fact, when the Ayatollah Khomeini, in exile before the Iranian Revolution in the 1970s, began to espouse his revolutionary theories of the Rule of the Jurisprudent (Velayat-e-Faqih), he turned Shi'ite thinking on its head in calling for an Islamic state in which the clerics would actually rule. As noted earlier, true to the long-held fears that such proximity could easily lead to the corruption of the clergy, that is what happened in the Islamic Republic of Iran, where corruption of the state clergy has been a major bane of the Iranian State.

Shi'a of course had come to power in various places and times in Muslim history, though usually in smaller local states and ruling dynasties, especially in the Indian sub-continent. The really major exception was the spectacular Fatimid Dynasty, an Isma'ili Shi'ite dynasty, which ruled from Cairo in a Caliphate that lasted for some 250 years beginning in 900 CE; it came to span all of North Africa and Red Sea coast of Arabia. It also produced some of the greatest glories of Islamic architecture in Cairo and elsewhere. All Arabs share in their pride of this Caliphate, despite its Shi'ite character—and indeed its "Shi'ite character" is usually overlooked or even forgotten in popular Sunni admiration for the Fatimids. The Shi'a never again attained major state power over such a large region for an enduring time until the 16th century in Iran—despite many smaller and often short-lived dynasties or families in southern India and in Iran.

Iran is popularly assumed to have "always" been a Shi'ite state, but the surprising fact is that it did not adopt Shi'ism as a state religion until as recently as 1500, when the Safavid Dynasty came to power. Anxious to assert their Persian distinctiveness against the dominant, powerful, Turkish-oriented—and Sunni—Ottoman Empire, the early Safavid rulers embraced Shi'ism to highlight their dramatic political difference from Ottoman power. Interestingly, at the time Persia was very poorly informed about Shi'ite practice. As a result, it was compelled to reach out to the distinguished body of Shi'ite clerics long resident in Lebanon. They supplied Iran with a group of religious scholars who could instruct the Iranian Sunni population in the basic principles of Shi'ite theology and practice. (Iran would return the favor under the Shah in the 1980s when it provided major stimulus to the downtrodden Lebanese Shi'ite community to organize their community anew in a striking recrudescence of Shi'ite power in Lebanon.) Persia/Iran has remained heavily Shi'ite ever since.

After officially adopting Shi'ism, the newly established Shi'ite state of Iran then fell into a 200-year cold war with the Ottoman Empire, each vilifying the other via harsh propaganda campaigns—accompanied by regular military conflict along the borders of the two empires. The intensity of this rivalry had markedly decreased by the mid-18th century, however. Typically the two empires in confrontation were driven largely by geopolitical considerations over regional power, influence, and territory. Since that highpoint of Ottoman-Iranian confrontations, geopolitical (and religious) conflicts between the two states markedly declined. In modern times their bilateral relations, while sometimes wary or prickly, have been strongly distinguished by a practical working relationship between them, at present for well over a century. Indeed, Iran has sometimes seen Turkey in many respects as a model for its own development (although far less so under the Islamic Republic).

HOW DOES IRAN FIGURE TODAY IN THE MAJOR SUNNI-SHI'ITE CONFLICTS OF THE REGION?

The Iran-Iraq Relationship
Today Iran still represents the major Shi'ite power in the Muslim world. But with the US invasion of Iraq, the overthrow of Saddam Hussein, and the

collapse of the long-time ruling Sunni elite, Iraq's Shi'a, in a portentous event, assumed dominance over national power. In every sense Iraq has now become the second most important Shi'ite state in the world. It is not officially a "Shi'ite state" however, nor will it be, since it of course contains a very large Sunni minority of both Arabs and Kurds.

Ever since the Iranian Revolution in 1979 and Saddam's subsequent invasion of Iran, Iran has lent moral, theological, and at times financial support to the Shi'ite community in Iraq, especially as it suffered persecution from Saddam's regime. Leading Iraqi Shi'ite clerics regularly took refuge in Iran, often escaping jail or death in Ba'thist Iraq. Many of these clerics were also schooled in Iran's religious institutions at Qom. With the fall of Saddam and the Sunni regime, however, most of these Iraqi clerics in exile returned to Iraq to play a major role in post-Saddam politics. Iran trained and often bankrolled several Shi'ite militias, many of which carried out resistance against the US military occupation of Iraq as well as asserting their power over Sunni militias. Iran has exerted major influence over the policies of the new Shi'ite-dominated government in Baghdad, though not unchallenged. We should not assume, however, that Iran will permanently exert major influence over Iraq. Indeed, over time Iraq may well emerge as a rival to Iran in the Persian Gulf on several grounds.

First, in historical terms, Iraq, and not Iran, has been the leading center of Shi'ism over long centuries, especially based in the two major shrines and theological centers of Najaf and Karbala. That is even truer today, now that Iraq has been liberated from Saddam's Sunni Ba'th Party rule.

The acknowledged leading Shi'ite theologian of the world is Grand Ayatollah 'Ali al-Sistani, who has long resided in Najaf and speaks out periodically on crucial political issues in Iraq. He is Iranian by birth (as his name indicates) but is deeply established in Iraqi culture and writes in Arabic. He is revered by a majority of Shi'ites around the world and of course in the Persian Gulf. Najaf and Karbala are shrine destinations for Shi'ite pilgrims far more than any comparable place in Iran, especially since the tomb of 'Ali himself is in Najaf. These facts lend Iraqi Shi'ism a special power.

As a result, it is nearly certain that Arab Shi'a in the Gulf will increasingly look to the new state of Iraq as a center of Shi'ism and the seat of major Ayatollahs. This comes at the expense of Iran, which will lose its former monopoly over theological issues relating to Shi'ism. Such a situation suggests the emergence of a clear rivalry between the two states for influence among Arab Shi'ite populations, and maybe beyond.

Some sense of solidarity among Iraqi Shi'a at present, however, is driven by feelings of insecurity; they are not yet confident that their emergence at the top of the political order is a permanent reality. Certainly the diplomatic reaction of Saudi Arabia, for example, has been to suggest there is something not quite legitimate about the new Shi'ite dominance of Iraqi politics. This insecurity has tended to push Iraqi Shi'a more deeply into unwise sectarian politics, moving to consolidate their power within the state at the expense of greater power-sharing and guarantees of Sunni community security. Over time, as the Iraqi Shi'a grow more confident about their position in Iraqi politics and society, chances are good that they will move toward a more inclusive order. It is, after all, in their interests to maintain their position over a united and stable Iraq rather than dominating—and contributing to—a divided and unstable Iraq.

Finally, most of the Shi'ite population on the Arab side of the Persian Gulf are themselves Arabs—although there are many big families of Iranian origin, now mostly Arabized. They more naturally look to Iraq as having the closest cultural links, and of course as the most important center of Shi'ism.

The "Shi'ite Threat"
What is the so-called "Shi'ite threat" that is so broadly invoked in the Gulf, most vigorously by Saudi Arabia? There is in fact a threat of sorts from Iran, though not in the way it is usually presented by Riyadh. The threat is actually more ideological and geopolitical than sectarian/religious.

First, the Iranian Revolution of 1979 is one of the genuine "revolutions" in modern times. Many countries in the Middle East have undergone military coups, palace coups, and power shifts, yet rarely anything reflecting the same widespread and deep social revolution that swept away the old order in Iran with the fall of the Shah. In the political and social turmoil following the flight of the Shah, the balance of politics in Iran was up for grabs with multiple popular movements on the right and the left struggling for power. In the end the Islamists managed to outmaneuver all other political forces and take power, bolstered by the triumphant return from exile of Grand Ayatollah Khomeini. Few other regional states have witnessed such a sweeping popular revolution; the event was admired with some envy by Arab populations in the region who felt still trapped in many of the old and seemingly immutable authoritarian Arab political orders.

Second, Khomeini's proclamation of an Islamic state represented a major ideological event in the Middle East. It represented perhaps the first serious intellectual effort to create a modern Islamic state with modern institutions while still reflecting Islamic values. The result was a striking blend of a basically democratic structure, a parliamentary process conducted by elected MPs, in addition to Islamic "oversight" carried out by several key committees to pass on the Islamic legitimacy of legislation, as a kind of Islamic Supreme Court. The very concept of calling the new Iranian state a "republic" represented a major ideological statement among Islamists, many of whom would have called a republic and a parliament "Western innovations."

A major shortcoming of Iran's democratic order—at least in the eyes of its liberal critics—was the ideological threshold that prospective candidates for Parliament needed to cross in order to qualify to run for office. This ideological screening resulted in a skewed system that heavily favored pro-regime and obviously religious candidates. Yet even within this context elections were hard fought; offered a significant range of candidates, meaningful debates; and the outcomes mattered a great deal in the evolving policies of the Islamic republic. Presidential elections in Iran have brought major change to national policies with each change of president. The country also enjoys a lively press with a considerable spectrum of debate, even though journalists are often jailed and newspapers are periodically closed down, often to reopen under a different name. Everything in the end depends on the tolerance of the Supreme Leader, that is, the supreme religious and political leader of the state who is appointed by a clerical council, not popularly elected.

In short, Iran has demonstrated something of a democratic process—albeit skewed—that is not to be found in most Arab states. It was, however, accompanied by socially restrictive laws on dress, public meetings, and elements of artistic expression. Opposition figures were often jailed. Still, taken as a whole, Iran's expression of a modern Islamic state offered a far greater dynamism with meaningful elements of democratic process than is present in most other regional states—apart from Turkey.

This stands in marked contrast to Saudi Arabia, which claims to be an Islamic state and whose constitution is the Qur'an. Needless to say, Saudi Arabia lacks even the most basic trappings of a modern democratic state or the intellectual and artistic openness, vigor, or dynamism of Iran.

The Islamic Republic of Iran also adopted a radical Islamic perspective of hostility toward kingship as an inappropriate form of Islamic governance. Islam has never promoted the idea of kingship as such; inherent in the root of the Arabic word for king—*malik*—is the suggestion of *possession* which does not accord with a just Islamic ruler's power, since that authority should remain contingent upon upholding of Islamic religious, social, and economic precepts, however defined. In reality, of course, kings, sultans, and emirs have been the dominant reality throughout Islamic history, as it has in the history of most of the rest of the world. Rule in Islam is made legitimate by just rule, consultation with the people, protection of Islamic lands and values. Contemporary regional monarchs nonetheless basically feel threatened by this critical approach to kingship in Islam.

Third, Iran extended its revolution to its foreign policy in its declaration of a universal vision of revolution, not just for Shi'ites but for all Muslims; indeed, at the outset of the revolution Iran claimed it was speaking for all the "oppressed of the earth"—clearly influenced by Third World revolutionary rhetoric. Furthermore, the Iranian Revolution has never declared itself a "Shi'ite revolution," but strictly an "Islamic Revolution." It never hesitated to embrace the quintessentially Sunni international Muslim Brotherhood as a sympathetic revolutionary Islamic force. It espoused the Palestinian cause as well, whose population is almost entirely Sunni, and has also supported Hamas, the Sunni militant wing of the Palestinian movement. Additionally, it has endorsed the Shi'ite Hizballah movement in Lebanon, another movement dedicated to resistance against Israel's power as well as the Israeli invasions and occupation of southern Lebanon in 1982. This Iranian support for resistance against Israeli power was widely admired by Arab public opinion at a time when most other Arab leaders were perceived as timid and unwilling to oppose the pro-Israel American policies in the Middle East.

Monarchies in the Gulf were also disturbed at the potential impact of revolutionary ideas on the Shi'ite populations living in the countries (shaykhdoms) of the Gulf. There are very significant Shi'ite minorities in every Gulf state, and in Bahrain the oppressed Shi'a constitute a dispossessed *majority*. The emergence of the Islamic Revolution and the Islamic Republic galvanized many of these minorities who hoped that the existence of the new Islamic Republic would bolster their own claims to greater rights within the states in which they lived, as well as lessen their oppression there.

During the 1978-1985 Iran-Iraq War, every one of the Gulf states and virtually every Arab state (except Syria and Algeria) fully supported Saddam Hussein's invasion of Iran with money and weapons after the Iranian Revolution. Faced with an existential threat, Iran in turn supported terrorist acts against the Gulf states in retribution. Iranian "subversion" in the Gulf largely came to an end after the end of the Iran-Iraq war, but many Gulf states, especially Saudi Arabia, continue to question the loyalty of Shi'a populations—which naturally sparks insecurity among the Shi'a populations under continuing discrimination. These suspicions of Shi'ite loyalty indeed contain elements of a self-fulfilling prophecy. Some Sunni Gulf Arabs actually refer to democracy as a "Shi'ite agenda," especially in Saddam's Iraq and in today's Bahrain—both places where they represent a majority. To be sure, Gulf state ruling elites believe that Shi'ite unhappiness and unrest is a product of Iranian agitation rather than a situation rooted in discriminatory local conditions.

Iran has been one of the few states in the Middle East to routinely defy US power and policies in the region—causing Washington to define it as a "rogue state." (In the Washington lexicon, a "rogue state" means a small state that openly resists the American blueprint for the regional order.) Iran's seemingly fearless stance against US power over the years is widely admired by Arab populations—though not by their rulers—for its gutsiness and courage. Syria, for over fifty years, has been the other major Arab state to pose long-term resistance to US dominance in the region—not because it is led by a quasi-Shi'ite leadership, but because it is strongly Arab nationalist.

45

Furthermore, outspoken Iranian resistance to the expansion of Israel—an obvious, yet self-willed US ally—into the Palestinian territories of the West Bank garners much popular support for Iran.

Meanwhile, Saudi Arabia has not been successful in promoting its own model of official state piety as expressed in its rigorous, even oppressive imposition of Wahhabi norms on daily life in the Kingdom. The Saudi reputation for hypocrisy among the ruling elite further undermines the Saudi claim to be a bulwark of Islam. The royal family is well known for its profligate and ostentatious lifestyle abroad in which gambling, drinking and womanizing make a mockery of Islamic public values and respect for Shari'a law. These problems are far less evident in Iran's own conservative public morality.

These, then, are some of the political grounds on which many of the Gulf rulers, and especially Saudi Arabia, believe Iran to pose an ideological threat to them, far more than any military threat. In fact Iran has not initiated war in over 200 years, so Tehran hardly offers a belligerent profile at the military level. That so many Gulf rulers claim to find Iran to be such a threat represents more a political rather than military or theological threat, and reflects their own insecurities. Intense Saudi dislike of Iran also stems from the particular religious precepts of Wahhabi Islam. (Qatar also identifies itself with "Wahhabism," but it expresses itself quite differently in a more open and tolerant society that enjoys generally good pragmatic relations with Iran.)

In sum, despite general Arab prejudice against Persians in general, there has been much widespread admiration for Iran as a strong self-confident, independent regional state willing to resist American pressures.

The Syrian conflict: The outbreak of an ugly civil war in Syria in 2011 was initially rooted in domestic issues and discontents but fairly rapidly took on the character of a complex and cross-cutting proxy war among the US, Iran, Iraq, Turkey, Saudi Arabia, and Russia, in addition to a number of minor players. Residual Arab popular admiration for Iran has receded with Iran's strong support for the now harsh and brutal Syrian regime of Bashar al-Asad. Turkey's President Erdoğan, once a mentor to Asad, turned against him when Asad refused to heed Turkey's advice and his fall appeared imminent. Erdoğan had initially hoped that a Muslim Brotherhood-dominated

Syria might emerge in place of Asad, closer to Erdoğan's liking. Iran's strong support for its long-time ally Asad is perceived by many as an anti-Sunni campaign, especially by Arab rulers and elites. Islamists and would-be democrats resent Iran's support for Asad's autocracy. Nonetheless Syria, for all its close ties to Iran over three decades, has almost never acted as a Shi'ite power, but as an Arab nationalist geopolitical power that has regularly supported Sunni radical causes and a number of Sunni Arab nationalist leaders.

With the fall of Sunni power in Iraq and its new domination by the Shi'a, Saudi Arabia decided to strike back by casting its antipathy to Iran in sweeping sectarian terms across the region. Riyadh called for a united Muslim front against Iran and has so far created deep cleavages in the region that were not strongly evident over the past many decades. It pits the Saudi state—a representative of the forces of the reactionary past in Middle East governance—against forces in Iran that are somewhat more representative of future regional governance: non-sectarianism against sectarianism and a trend towards democracy rather than authoritarianism. In this regard, Turkey is not a natural ally of Saudi Arabia, either, despite all of Riyadh's efforts to enlist Ankara in the anti-Shi'ite campaign. Turkey represents the forces of globalization, non-sectarianism, soft-power, democratic institutions, and secularism. Saudi Arabia stands for the exact antithesis.

In effect, Iran is offering a contemporary version (still evolving) of an Islamic state that directly challenges the Saudi model whose main claim to Islamic legitimacy is its custodianship of the two holy places of Mecca and Medina. Indeed, the Saudi king uses this as his chief legitimizing designation, not the title of King of Saudi Arabia.

The royal family's Wahhabism is furthermore deeply hostile to the Sufism (Islamic mysticism) present in the Sunni tradition, but especially strong in the Shi'ite tradition. Wahhabism detests any suggestion of an intermediary between the individual and God; hence almost any shrine to any saint (including the Prophet Muhammad himself) is considered blasphemous and to be destroyed.

Lebanon: The Shi'a in southern Lebanon have been poor and oppressed for centuries under Sunni rule. Yet beginning in the 1980s, the Lebanese Shi'a, who constitute the single largest community in Lebanon, built up their communal power with Iranian help and created a powerful militia, Hizballah. Hizballah has impressed all Arabs with the courage and commitment of its resistance against the Israeli invasion of Lebanon on several occasions. Today Hizballah represents a major political and social as well as military force in Lebanon; it is deeply integrated into Lebanese politics. Iran's support has strengthened it, but it is not a creature of Iran and is solidly rooted in Lebanese society. Saudi Arabia, however, views Lebanon as yet another place where Iran has conspired to strengthen Shi'ite forces against the Saudis' preferred clients there.

Yemen: Yemen is a fourth major site of Iranian-Saudi geopolitical rivalry, especially after Yemen was struck by Arab Spring rebellions. Clear Sunni-Shi'ite lines are not easily drawn in this conflict, however. For the time being the victorious power in Yemen is the Huthi clan, a major Zaydi ("Fiver" Shi'ite) tribe. They rebelled against the policies of another Zaydi leader, Yemen's former president of 23 years, who had been under heavy Saudi influence. Riyadh has accused Iran of backing the Huthi rebellion, which by the end of 2015 had taken over most of the country. Although Iran has indeed given some rhetorical support to the Huthis, as well as probably some limited military support to be used against Saudi military intervention in Yemen, few political observers consider Iran's modest contribution to the Huthi rebellion to have meaningful military significance.

Nonetheless Riyadh perceives Iran's marginal involvement as part of a "Shi'ite encirclement" of the Kingdom and has subsequently conducted a brutal air war against Yemen since 2014 in order to restore its own preferred leader. Civilian deaths reached 300,000 in mid-2016, with over two and a half million people displaced. Saudi Arabia has always considered its domination of Yemen to be an essential part of Saudi geopolitical strategy; for decades it has dispersed lavish funds to maintain its preferred leadership in Yemen despite widespread popular hostility against Saudi Arabia.

Bahrain: Bahrain has been the fifth arena of confrontation between Riyadh and Tehran. Although the Shi'a of Bahrain constitute some 60 to 70 percent of the population, the Sunni ruling al-Khalifa family has consistently discriminated against the Shi'a and excluded them from a voice in governing.

Periodic uprisings by Shi'a in demand of greater rights and freedoms have been frequent for decades. In 2011, when the Arab Spring sparked yet a new phase of anti-Khalifa agitation and rioting in Bahrain, the al-Khalifa called for Saudi Arabia to send troops to put the uprising down. Saudi troops have been there ever since, a situation criticized even by many Western leaders, including the UN Secretary-General Ban Ki-moon. Iran over the years has consistently lent vocal support to the oppressed Shi'ite community. The ruling al-Khalifas have regularly accused Iran of fomenting the troubles and arming the low-key uprising. While Iran has contacts with some of the top leadership of the Bahraini opposition movement, there is little evidence that the uprising is anything but a local uprising against long-time oppressive anti-Shi'a policies. Bahrain, an island connected to the Saudi mainland by a causeway, is now effectively under Saudi domination. The close family ties that exist between Bahraini Shi'a clans and the Shi'ite clans of the eastern province of Saudi Arabia, create additional anxiety for Riyadh, fearing its own restive and oppressed Shi'ite population. The Bahrain situation strengthens Riyadh's anxieties regarding encirclement by an Iran-orchestrated Shi'ite threat.

★ ★ ★

In the final analysis it is hard to escape the conclusion that it is the Sunnis who have a problem with Shi'ite Islam, rather than Shi'a having a problem with Sunni Islam. Sunnis fundamentally view all Shi'a as illegitimate and rawafidh, or "rejecters," of the mainstream Sunni tradition from early on. Sunni fundamentalists view them as worse than any non-Muslim threat since they represent an internal schism. Still, there is little that Shi'a living in a Sunni society can do to remedy their problem. When the Shi'a suppress their Shi'ite identity and try to integrate into Sunni society they are viewed as "infiltrating" and have their Shi'ite identity thrown at them. When they call for equal treatment as Shi'ites and insist on their Shi'ite identity, then their loyalty to the state is challenged as a threat to the whole "Sunni narrative" of history.

Tensions between Shi'a and Sunni have varied greatly over history. Yet there is reason to believe that the present state of tensions, now largely exacerbated and exploited by Saudi Arabia, will eventually decline again with time.

What is more urgent is that Muslim politics must shift its ground: ethnic, religious, and sectarian identities ultimately must give way to other social identities as the chief element of political and social discourse. Transient and optional identities—professional, class, economic, political, and ideological—need to become the primary arena for political debates, as in most countries, rather than factors of religion and ethnicity which are not optional and are immutable.

In the coming decades Turkey and Iran are the two major regional powers that fundamentally do not self-identify or promote themselves as Sunni or Shi'ite states, and which will likely be the key external players in the politics in the Arab world around them. Iran and/or Turkey (and even eventually Iraq) could well come to play the key role in adjudicating the fate of the smaller Persian Gulf shaykhdoms. This will be especially relevant in the face of a potentially resurgent and expansionist Saudi state in the future—particularly one driven by the narrow and intolerant expansionist vision of Wahhabism that has sent its militant forces twice in two centuries against the populations of the Gulf, right up to Basra and Karbala in Iraq.

It is in this context that Saudi Arabia, as the regional bastion of Wahhabism/ Salafism, perceives the greater political and social flexibility of Shi'ism and even Sufism (Sunni and Shi'i) to be a major challenge and threat to the narrowness and rigidity of Saudi doctrine that represents the ideological underpinnings of the Saudi state. The mere existence of Shi'ism as a different sect embodies an alternative in Islam that is not acceptable to the deeply unitarian (tawhidi) Saudi approach to Islam, which accepts no straying from its view of the one true path. Riyadh has furthermore been willing to support violent jihadi groups outside of Saudi Arabia to further its Islamic agenda.

More than in just theological terms, though, Iran also poses a political and ideological threat to Saudi Arabia as Riyadh sees it. It has taken political positions in the Middle East that are popular among the masses—both Sunni and Shi'i alike—offering an outspokenness which rulers beholden to the West feel they cannot do. Thus Iran is outspoken on the plight of the Palestinians; some Iranians (and non-Iranians) suggest that a Jewish state that excludes or discriminates against Palestinians is not a legitimate state in the Middle East. Iran has called for an end to the Zionist state, though not to drive Jews into the sea as is commonly interpreted. Rather—much as many in the US had called for an end to the Communist state in Russia and not the destruction of the Russian people—so, too, Iran wants an end to the present Israeli Zionist and racially oriented state as opposed to a binational one. Iran has similarly dared to stand up to US power—even defy the US in many respects—in ways that few other leaders in the region would dare do, even if their own populations wanted it. In effect, through its political positions Iran offers an alternative, contemporary view of Muslim *power* that has appeal despite its Shi'ite character.

And of course Iran represents a rival in regional oil and gas production and pricing; yet in this respect Iran is just one of many oil (and gas) states involved in contentious pricing issues.

In the final analysis, therefore, it is misleading to analyze the harsh sectarian war in the Middle East today as either permanent or as representing the essence of the conflict. Actual theology has little to do with it, even though Riyadh has chosen to propagate its geopolitical struggle in theological terms. This Saudi strategy is dangerous and destabilizing and has led to the strengthening of extremist jihadist groups such as al-Qa'ida and ISIS and civil conflict in Pakistan, Iraq, Syria, Yemen, Bahrain, Lebanon, and elsewhere. It is high time to abandon these camouflage ideologies and look to solutions for the real geopolitical and (non-religious) ideological issues at stake.

Islamic State (ISIS)

The "Islamic State" in Syria and Iraq (also known as ISIS, ISIL or *Da'ish*) represents an extraordinary chapter in the history of modern Islamist movements. At a time when it appeared that al-Qa'ida represented the most extreme and violent movement in modern times, the phenomenon of ISIS has exceeded it in ideological, strategic, territorial, and tactical reach.

ISIS would not of course exist were it not for the US invasion of Iraq and the overthrow of the Ba'th regime there. ISIS first emerged under the name of "al-Qa'ida in Iraq," where its first task was to fight the US occupation. This task represented a new opportunity for al-Qa'ida headquarters in Afghanistan since it had previously lacked a significant presence in Iraq. Resistance to the US military presence would provide a popular cause.

While both al-Qa'ida and ISIS are jihadi organizations, the differences between them are nonetheless striking and rest on personal, tactical, and ideological foundations. Abu Mus'ab al-Zarqawi, the founder of al-Qa'ida in Iraq, and of what was to become ISIS, revealed early disagreement with al-Qa'ida, particularly with 'Usama bin Laden's deputy leader Ayman al-Zawahiri. There were five crucial differences between them.

First, al-Zarqawi, as an operative in Iraq, demonstrated intense anti-Shi'ite feelings; this was especially so after Iraq's Shi'ite majority came to power in free elections, after the US invasion overthrew Saddam Hussein. While al-Qa'ida itself is theologically hostile to Shi'a on religious grounds, it opposed wholesale gratuitous alienation of the Shi'a at a time when al-Qa'ida sought to gain a foothold in Iraq.

Second, al-Qa'ida advised Zarqawi to be less violent in his general treatment of other Muslims. It opposed the lurid violence portrayed in ISIS videos, public beheadings, and other gruesome forms of execution that could alienate the general public and drive them away from the movement. Zarqawi and his successors, on the other hand, believed that policies of "shock and awe," compulsion and fear, rather than suasion, would be the most effective means of gaining and maintaining control over populations.

Third, al-Zarqawi had a vision of *territorial control* within distinct borders, something which al-Qa'ida had never done. Al-Qa'ida saw no urgency for the proclamation of an Islamic State until conditions were ripe, when there would be strong public backing for such a move. Zarqawi, however, believed in the importance of creating a specific territorial presence on the ground. Al-Qa'ida had never established a territorial quasi-state presence.

Fourth, al-Qa'ida felt it was highly premature to proclaim a Caliphate, as Zarqawi proposed. Again, it believed the conditions were not ripe, and the public not ready for such a step, nor did it represent a priority goal, compared to the need of building strong cadres and driving the US out of Iraq.

Fifth, Al-Qa'ida opposed the creation of ISIS as a movement independent of itself and hoped to keep it subordinate to al-Qa'ida.

Zarqawi was killed in 2006 by a US strike. His successors immediately declared an Islamic State, contrary to al-Qa'ida's preferences. Abu Bakr al-Baghdadi eventually took over the movement and declared himself Caliph—a major ideological precedent in jihadi history. Unlike 'Usama bin Laden, who was largely a self-taught student of Islamic law, Baghdadi had a doctorate in Islamic studies from the University of Baghdad. He had even considered proclaiming himself "the Mahdi," the final Islamic ruler who will emerge in the apocalyptic conditions of the End of Days.

In terms of arguing for the establishment of a Caliphate, there is only one other main group which has seriously examined in detail the issues involved in establishing the political architecture of a modern Caliphate: Hizbut Tahrir (Hizb al-Tahrir, or Liberation Party). This group is a movement rather than a political party; it is based in the UK but with worldwide affiliates, especially in Central Asia. It is pan-Islamic in outlook, looking for the ulti-mate creation of a single global Islamic State. It produces a great variety of literature and public statements. It is technically a non-violent movement that preaches highly conservative social Islam and seeks to slowly build a mass following that will one day form the foundation of an expanding Islamic State and Caliphate. Hizbut Tahrir, as a non-terrorist organization, is legal in many countries in the West. It, too, is hostile to ISIS on numerous tactical, political, and ideological issues, apart from sharing the goal of an ultimate overarching Islamic State under a Caliphate.

The nearest likely equivalent to ISIS at the moment may be Boko Haram, a murderous movement based in northern Nigeria that controls some shifting back-country territory and proclaims itself an Islamic Emirate. Its politics are intimately tied up in regional struggle, local politics, tribes, gangs, and crime, and it has a similar record of gruesome slaughter of civilians. Boko Haram recently declared its allegiance to ISIS, but in the main this step is best seen as an opportunistic effort to trade on the ISIS "brand."

When ISIS first came to major international attention during the jihadi struggle against the US occupation of Iraq and proceeded towards building a state, its rapid conquests and establishment of a crude but functional working state were astonishing. It thrived on the chaos and turmoil of post-Saddam Iraq. It gained a large pool of professional cadres from ex-Ba'th Party officials, former Iraqi military officers, as well as from jihadi and anti-US resistance groups and from anti-Shi'ite groups who opposed the new Shi'ite-dominated government, despite its legitimate election.

A second contributing factor to the rapid rise of ISIS was the outbreak of civil war in Syria in 2011, which provided the political and social turmoil in which ISIS could develop a base and draw on anti-Asad Sunni forces struggling against the nominally Shi'ite regime of Bashar al-Asad. Unlike in Iraq, neither the US or Europe could be seen as directly responsible for the Syrian civil war; blame here must be laid squarely at the door of Bashar al-Asad himself and his brutal suppression of anti-regime protests from the early days.

A third factor contributing to the unusual character of ISIS is the apocalyptic character of the movement: its choreographed, grisly executions filmed with great professionalism, along with its frequent apocalyptic invocation of the End Times. The overall violence of the Syrian civil war and the Iraqi internal struggle also helped create an apocalyptic mood; such an environment posed some attraction to disillusioned Muslim youth who felt drawn to participating in a polarizing moment in the history of Islam and the anti-Western struggle. Indeed, ISIS has characterized US and Western forces in the region as the "New Crusaders," lending a deeper sense of religious struggle between Islam and the West. ISIS describes these forces as a coalition of Jews and Christians fighting under the banner of the Antichrist against Islam. These represent emotive concepts to impressionable minds. Even the name of the slick ISIS publication, *Dabiq*, refers to a town in Syria associated with the Apocalypse.

All this might have gone on largely outside of public attention and interest, within the borders of Iraq and Syria, and without engaging the West. It was the theatrical violence as well as the filmed hideous executions of especially Western hostages, however, which helped propel the US and the West into direct engagement in the struggle against ISIS. Finally, of course, ISIS' sudden recourse to major terrorist operations in the West made it nearly impossible for the West to avoid turning to some military means to degrade, and destroy, ISIS.

IS ISIS ISLAMIC?

This question is highly politicized, and the answer depends on viewpoint and even on political agenda.

Yes, ISIS is Islamic. Al-Baghdadi, with his doctorate in Islamic Law, is better educated in Islam theology than any other political leader in the Middle East today. Nearly all of ISIS' actions are justified in terms of certain texts in the Qur'an and the Hadith (sayings and doings of the Prophet.) These texts are consistent with radical readings of Salafism or Wahhabism. They are of course also highly selective, sometimes subject to dubious interpretation, taken out of context, or represent an outmoded interpretation that would be rejected by nearly all Muslims today, such as issues of execution of non-Muslims, slavery, and especially sexual slavery—part of warfare since the dawn of creation. Baghdadi did not just invent these things.

But no, ISIS is not Islamic. It does not represent the kind of Islam supported by the vast majority of Muslims in the world today. It does not represent the kind of society in which Muslims wish to live. Above all, it violates the spirit of Islam. Even Bin Laden and his successor Ayman al-Zawahiri criticized violence—at least on a pragmatic basis. For most Muslims and scholars of Islam it is not enough to cite narrowly and selectively from holy texts. There is a need for a broad interpretation of Islam. The texts of nearly all religions in certain places have terrible things to say about the use of violence, the treatment of enemies and apostates. All religions are used to justify violence as well as peace. The Old Testament is filled with warfare, vengeance, and brutal punishments along with inspiring poetry and high moral vision. The famous Pakistani Islamic scholar Fazlur Rahman stressed that you cannot look just at the *text*, you must look at the *context* of passages in the Qur'an or the Hadith in order to grasp the true meaning.

This question of whether ISIS is truly Islamic is not just academic but has significant consequences. The question is also highly politicized, depending upon the *intent or agenda* lying behind the response. Some Islamophobic groups and xenophobes in the West with their own political agendas insist on ISIS' Islamic nature. They wish to project a vision of Islam that is so violent and primitive that it has no place in the modern world and cannot be negotiated with. They strongly argue that Islam itself represents a regression, a threat to the civilized world in which ISIS is exhibit number one in their search for evidence to promote their views.

Progressives, on the other hand, who seek reconciliation with Islam and the Muslim world in general, respond (rightfully in my view) that ISIS is not truly representative of Islam, even if it draws from specific texts here and there for justification. They argue that ISIS strongly contradicts the spirit of the Faith. They seek inclusion, dialog, reconciliation, and cooperation between Muslim communities and the West. They argue that the grounds for finding common cause between religions clearly exist and must be the focus of attention—not the differences. ISIS should therefore not be taken as essentially Islamic in character. A search for *differences* between cultures deliberately leads to conflict. A search for commonality leads to reconciliation.

THE APPEAL OF ISIS

How could a movement that is so harsh, violent, narrow, and uncompromising win any kind of support from outside?

We have already noted a number of novel factors about ISIS that have drawn attention to it. The use of symbolic terms, like the "Islamic State" or the Caliphate, possess historical and cultural power; these terms suggest a dynamic new look in Muslim politics at a time when the region is dominated by sclerotic, tired, corrupt, and ineffective regimes. For disillusioned and unemployed youth who feel they have nothing to live for, ISIS offers excitement, a modern cause, positive action, a riposte to the West that has been oppressing them. It offers a vehicle of action to those Sunnis who feel oppressed under the minority regime of Bashar al-Asad—although Asad has actually always been a champion of many Sunni causes like Arab nationalism and the Palestinian cause. ISIS dramatically rejects the Western-imposed borders of the imperial Sykes-Picot agreement and proclaims the advent of an expanding Islamic state unhindered by the borders of the old imperial order. It is willing to take on the West, stand up to Western power, even export its own asymmetric power and strike back at the West. It suggests the foundations of a new cultural and moral power, based on the precepts of Islam, the region's religious and cultural heritage. True, it is violent, but such movements always rationalize early violence as a necessary stage of destruction in order to give birth to something new, creative and constructive. Herein lies the appeal of ISIS to some—admittedly narrow—elements of the Muslim population.

INTERNATIONAL ASPECTS OF THE ISIS CONFLICT

As we noted, ISIS was born out of the cataclysms in Iraq, starting with the resistance movement against the US occupation in 2003. This is only one of the many international forces that now surround ISIS. Indeed, it has become the focus of many growing proxy wars in the region that have placed it at the center of broader international struggle.

The US, now a key player in the struggle, has been consistently ambivalent about how to respond to the ISIS challenge, particularly since it did not wish to become involved in another Middle Eastern ground war. There had been many gruesome killings and executions in Iraq and Syria after the founding of the Islamic State, overwhelmingly involving Muslim victims. Multiple events gradually pushed Washington and other Western powers into the conflict, though. Various ISIS outrages had captured the attention of the Western media, including wholesale slaughter of minorities in the Middle East, the introduction of sexual slavery, and the destruction of cultural heritage monuments. It was ISIS terrorist operations in the West, however, that tipped the Western policy balance. In 2014 various operations, apparently carried out by "lone wolf" actors inspired by ISIS, took place in several countries including France, the US, Canada, and Australia. In 2015 the scale of such operations greatly increased, particularly in France and Belgium, but also against other states such as Russia, Turkey, Tunisia, and Lebanon.

Despite these operations and outrages, Washington remained ambivalent about what course to follow. ISIS, after all, had also been fighting to overthrow the Asad regime, a US goal as well. So for many months Washington was undecided on policy; this situation changed only when it grew clear that radical jihadi forces in Syria unfortunately represented more effective fighting forces against the Asad regime than did the so-called moderates or "moderate jihadis." The very battlefield effectiveness of ISIS therefore raised the inescapable question about what the character of any successor to the Asad regime might be. Gradually President Obama came to the conclusion that however much Washington hated Asad, any successor regime would quite likely be more radical, destabilizing, and anti-Western than Asad himself; indeed ISIS could help implant a radical jihadi government in power in Damascus.

Yet there is a longer history to US opposition to Asad; it did not begin in 2011 with the anti-Asad uprisings. Washington has always disliked both Bashar al-Asad, along with his father Hafiz before him, and has consistently sought to weaken them politically through various means, including covert operations and cooperation with Israel going back nearly fifty years. The Asads were perceived as a force representing Arab nationalism, resistance against Western power in the region, anti-imperialism, anti-Westernism, support for the Palestinian cause, and hostility toward Israel's expanding power. (Ironically, both father and son were also committed secularists.) Syria had consistently been a key Russian client during the Cold War. Thus the Arab Spring uprisings were seen by many in Washington, especially neo-conservative ideologists, as a chance to complete unfinished business. Washington had as a result found itself drawn into supporting certain so-called moderate anti-Asad forces (some were indeed politically moderate but militarily ineffective).

The entry of Russian air and ground forces into Syria in September 2015 changed the game markedly—an event over which Washington agonized. Washington policy circles have been largely dominated by those who perceive any Russian gain in the region as an automatic American loss and strongly oppose any Russian role there. Others, though, including some even in the Pentagon, believe that Moscow and Washington share many common goals, including the elimination of ISIS and jihadi terrorism. President Putin, determined to prevent the fall of Damascus to jihadi forces, declared that all jihadi forces are part of the greater problem—and that they threaten even Russia itself in its own large Muslim areas. Moscow therefore began to attack all jihadi forces, even those supposedly moderate fighting forces supported by Turkey, Saudi Arabia, and the US. US-Russian rivalry in Syria remains an underlying factor in events, although both states have worked to cooperate as much as possible to bring about an end to the conflict.

Other geopolitical ambitions also infect the ISIS struggle. Turkish president Erdoğan, once a close mentor to Asad, grew angered by 2012 at Asad's failure to heed Turkish advice towards moderation in Asad's brutal (and unwise) handling of the Syrian civilian opposition. Erdoğan also was sympathetic to the possibility of a Muslim Brotherhood government coming to power in Damascus, but this remained a retreating dream as more radical Islamist forces took the lead in the anti-Asad struggle, displacing the Brotherhood and other more moderate Islamist forces. Since then Erdoğan had grown obsessed with the overthrow of Asad and went all out to support anti-Asad forces, including even quietly permitting weapons and Western jihadi fighters to flow through Turkey to ISIS and to allow oil from ISIS territory to enter Turkish territory. But several major terrorist incidents against Turkey by ISIS, as well as unremitting pressure from the US, ultimately caused Ankara to reconsider this policy. Indeed, Erdoğan's strong anti-Asad policies brought it into confrontation not just with the US but with Iran, Iraq, and Russia as well, largely destroying Ankara's theretofore successful "good neighbor policy." These policies also drove Erdoğan into an unwise (and probably transient) alliance with Saudi Arabia to bring down the Asad regime at any cost.

Saudi Arabia, too, in its efforts against Asad, has quietly supported radical jihadis linked to al-Qa'ida, despite the fact that both al-Qa'ida and ISIS perceive the Kingdom as their sworn enemy. Saudi Arabia is more driven by its obsessive desire to checkmate Iran on any and every issue and hence devotes more attention to overthrowing Asad (as a significant Iranian ally) rather than to the destruction of ISIS itself.

Iran in turn is determined to keep Asad in power in order to prevent anti-Iranian Sunni jihadis from taking power in Damascus, and to block Riyadh's efforts to create a Sunni coalition against Iran's position in the region—a sworn Saudi goal. Iraq with its Shi'ite-dominated government (since the fall of Saddam Hussein) is similarly determined to prevent Saudi-backed radical jihadis from overthrowing a friendly regime in Syria.

Finally, the turmoil in Syria has produced massive human dislocation and a refugee flow out of the country that has spilled over heavily into Europe. Apart from the mainly Muslim victims from the ISIS regime in the Middle East, the "collateral damage" of the Syrian war in Europe has been extremely serious. It has created huge policy quarrels; damaged EU governing procedures and border protocols; sparked anti-Muslim and anti-refugee emotions and backlash; and helped revitalize right-wing, xenophobic, and neo-fascist movements across the EU. This structural damage to Europe may be the single most dangerous effect of ISIS over the longer term. And whereas most Western military intervention in the Middle East in recent decades has been unadvised and counterproductive, the damage now to Europe itself provides some of the most compelling argumentation in favor of Western military operations to help bring about an early end to ISIS as an "Islamic State"— that is, as a geographical entity.

PROSPECTS FOR ISIS

As of November 2016, it seems that the future of ISIS faces severe constraints. It has lost major territorial holdings, especially in areas near the Turkish border, and the loss of the major cities of Fallujah with Mosul, Iraq's second largest city, on the brink of collapse. It is likely it will cease to exist as a "state" within one year. The reasons are many. It has never truly been a "real" state. It has no recognized permanent borders. It has gained no diplomatic recognition from any other state, nor does it practice anything resembling "foreign relations" with other states, only with other jihadi groups. It does seem to have developed a few working arrangements with some regional states—if only unspoken and certainly unpublicized—such as Turkey and Saudi Arabia, with which it shares common anti-Asad ambitions.

ISIS is increasingly isolated. The flow of outsiders in support of the "Islamic State" seems to be diminishing, as its true character is becoming better known. Its economy is dwindling as its lines of communication with the world beyond become increasingly circumscribed, thereby damaging that economy. The economy itself is primarily based on temporary plunder of resources, extortion, and taxation, in addition to covert shipment of oil outside the country—an avenue that is increasingly cut off. It also receives some funding from private citizens in the Gulf. Western bomb attacks against ISIS troops, headquarters, infrastructure, logistical centers, and economic installations have further damaged it. Citizens who live within it find life increasingly harsh and dangerous and many seek to flee. ISIS laws and strictures are harsh to its population.

Regional states and forces are now arrayed against it, including Iraq and Syria, Iran, and Hizballah's forces in Lebanon. External western forces such as the US, Canada, and several European states are active in the military campaign. The subsequent addition of Russian forces to the anti-ISIS coalition has particularly turned the tide as ISIS loses key cities and centers. Its militias seek to migrate to new locations, such as Libya or Afghanistan. Its days are clearly numbered, although ultimately it will require ground troops—almost certainly non-Western ones—to eliminate the last of its strongholds, especially its major prize, Mosul.

ISIS AND THE FUTURE

The ISIS phenomenon may represent a significant turning point in the history of jihadi Islam. It seems hard to imagine that a yet more radical Islamic movement could come into being, at least in terms of harshly interpreting the more extreme precepts and interpretations of the Qur'an and the Hadith on the ground and in society. That is not to say that there cannot be anything more violent or destructive. It is always possible that some apocalyptic group might gain control of nuclear materials and could create a dirty bomb that would spread radioactive material over a limited space. These kinds of activities, however, lie more in the realm of the criminal rather than the political. Countering such groups and operations requires the same kind of police work as surveilling and spotting of any criminal organization.

More important, though, is the impact of the ISIS phenomenon on Muslims themselves. They are the first victims of ISIS and other acts of terrorism in the name of Islam—in two respects. First, they are overwhelmingly the primary victims of terrorism in terms of numbers in the Middle East itself—both Sunnis and Shi'a. Second, when such terrorist events take place, especially in the West, it is the Muslim community that pays the price of greater suspicion, discrimination, and surveillance. Thus Muslim communities themselves are increasingly compelled to police their own communities, if they feel that an individual or individuals betray signs of attraction to radical jihadism or terrorist operations that threaten the welfare of the community as a whole.

Put another way, are there "natural limits" to the violence and extremism that the expression of jihadi Islam can achieve? As of now it would seem unlikely that newer, even more radical interpretations of Islam could emerge, or that yet more radical jihadi organizations would appear on the ground, especially in the West. It is unlikely that any such organizations would exert a broad force of attraction upon the greater Muslim community, whatever the justification.

The failure of ISIS—its own disastrous mistakes and extremism, coupled with a growing array of Muslim and non-Muslim powers against it—will represent an important milestone. It will never again be easy for a successor group to come up once again with the idea of a Caliphate, or a borderless Islamic state, or harsh imposition of Shari'a law, that would lend it sudden, new appeal. The novelty of the ISIS experience cannot be indefinitely repeated, and the Muslim world will inevitably grow more cynical and experienced with the outcomes of such apocalyptic experiments. It is doubtful that the ISIS experience can ever be quite duplicated with the same degree of attraction and spectacular character elsewhere as it is today on Iraqi-Syrian soil. Violent jihadism has perhaps reached its apogee of appeal in Muslim *public perception*. Once the ideological appeal is diminished, it becomes more of a criminal problem.

This is not to say that terrorism itself has now reached its natural limits and will subsequently diminish. It will not—particularly in the Middle East, where radical and violent conditions have never been at such a consistently high level. Ongoing wars, civil struggles, sectarian clashes, chaos, anarchy, breakdown of the economic and social structures—all are at an all-time high in modern history. The key to beginning to eliminate extremism lies in the restoration of some degree of social and political order, well-regulated society, and the existence of trusted, effective authority. Such a state will not come about until all external intervention comes to an end, particularly from the West. That is the indispensable beginning for the restoration of some degree of *calm*. Nor will calm come right away with the departure of Western boots on the ground; that is only the prerequisite. Anger and frustration will take time to subside. Furthermore, local warfare is likely to continue in many parts of the Muslim world—as of course elsewhere in the world as well. Such local conflict may be highly disruptive. Overtones of East-West conflict or the suggestion of a "civilizational war" against Islam may start to ring more hollow. Time is required for some degree of political and social peace to return. Still, the first step requires an end to the West's incessant role in intervention.

ISIS itself will likely metastasize to other areas of the Muslim world as well. It already has in its small presence in Afghanistan, where it is in direct competition and conflict with the Taliban—an entirely different order of fundamentalist movement. The Taliban are about Afghan politics, along with the struggle of Pashtun nationalists to regain power in the country. It is a "traditional" form of political struggle, even if it assumes some degree of Islamic rhetoric to justify its essentially nationalistic campaign. ISIS has also established a few bridgeheads in Libya, although they remain under local siege.

In the end, *local* radical jihadi movements are far more likely to succeed or prosper than transnational ones that are not in touch with the local political aspirations of the broader public. In these respects, for instance, ISIS in Libya faces the rivalry of other established local movements who know the turf and have a stake in the deep-rooted politics of the region. ISIS cannot easily compete with such groups over the longer term. Similarly, while Boko Haram in Africa now claims loyalty to ISIS, the dynamic of Boko Haram is entirely different and is limited to a specific part of Africa where a complex of negative conditions are local and ripe for such violence.

In effect, these issues raise the broader and more fundamental question of whether it is ever possible to eliminate political violence and terrorism from the world. The answer is, of course, no. Sadly, political violence seems part of the human condition. Yet that does not mean that the world cannot achieve some degree of reduction of the phenomenon. Nonetheless, as long as there are major political and social grievances anywhere, people will invariably seek and find *vehicles through which to express them.*

We can recall the history of socialism, a widely popular political, social, and economic ideology for over a century. Yet that ideal was carried to an extreme with concepts of Marxism, then Leninism, and then Stalinism, in a state-run movement of political violence that ended up murdering some 20 million people in the name of applied communism and the elimination of whole social classes. The ideal reached yet newer levels of extremism, violence, and death under the communism of China's Mao Zedong, resulting in probably 40 million deaths through various regime-induced causes over the years. The apocalyptic, blind, and fanatic brutality of Pol Pot in Cambodia, too, saw the ultimate in mass genocide of a nearly psychotic form of "communism."

In short, any religion or ideology can be driven to extremes of violence and killing. In the Middle East it is hardly surprising that Islamic ideas should create the foundation for political movements with a "native ring" to them in many different forms. Right now, in ISIS, it happens to reach its most extreme form. Yet it still reflects to a great degree the particular political, geopolitical, economic, social, religious, and environmental conditions of today's Middle East that remain highly negative. Those conditions can and will eventually change. Extremism will then begin to find less fertile soil.